# THE UNTAMED GARDEN AND
# OTHER PERSONAL ESSAYS

# THE UNTAMED GARDEN AND OTHER PERSONAL ESSAYS

*DAVID RAINS WALLACE*

*ILLUSTRATIONS BY JULIE S. LEECH*

 A SANDSTONE BOOK

Ohio State University Press : Columbus

"The End of the Earth" and "Wetlands in America" (under another title) appeared originally in *Wilderness* (Spring 1984 and Winter 1985 issues respectively); they are reprinted here by permission.

"The Nature of Nature Writing" appeared originally in the *New York Times Book Review,* 22 July 1984. Copyright © 1984 by the New York Times Company. Reprinted by permission.

"Gardening with Pests," "The Mind of the Beaver," "Ravens," "The Importance of Predators," and "The Untamed Garden" appeared earlier in *Blair & Ketchum's Country Journal.*

Many of the essays in this volume appeared over a period of many months in a column entitled "The Naturalist" in the *Berkeley Monthly.*

**Library of Congress Cataloguing in Publication Data**
Wallace, David Raines, 1945–
  The untamed garden and other personal essays.

  "A Sandstone book."
  1. Natural history.   2. Ecology.   3. Garden ecology.
I. Title.
QH81.W26   1986                     508                     86-21667
ISBN 0-8142-0423-6

To Mark Osaki

# Contents

# III  Natural History and Conservation

# IV  Wildlife

# Foreword

DAVID Rains Wallace's four books have established him firmly in the front rank of naturalist writers. *The Dark Range, Idle Weeds, The Klamath Knot,* and the ecological mystery *The Turquoise Dragon* provide abundant evidence that Wallace is a sensitive and alert student of the natural world and that he writes evocatively and imaginatively about that world. This volume, the first collection of his occasional essays, will demonstrate that he brings the same qualities to this equally demanding shorter form. A few of these pieces were published in periodicals of national circulation, but most appeared in a San Francisco Bay Area monthly. This book will provide for Wallace's essays the wider audience they deserve.

It is never easy to define precisely the qualities that distinguish a genuinely unusual writer or a unique literary accomplishment. The most determined analyst inevitably comes to the point of having to acknowledge, overtly or implicitly, that there is a mystery in the author or the work that analysis cannot fathom; this is, I think, akin to the mystery that the scientist-naturalist confronts in his or her investigations of natural phenomena, and it deserves the same respect. So in the essays of David Rains Wallace, there is a point at which the analyst must simply lay aside the tools of his trade and say, "I cannot fully explain this; I can only say that it works wonderfully well."

Before reaching that point, however, there are qualities in these essays that can be defined, qualities that provide a basis for the reader's admiration. First among these is one that Wallace shares with other students of the natural world: his close observation of phenomena, which he combines with the rarer ability to convey vividly the results of that observation. The contents of an artificial lake in the heart of a large city, the animal population of a compost heap, or the habits of that generally despised bird the starling, all are observed acutely and described with consistent clarity and grace. When Wallace introduces such a mundane topic as puddles, we learn not only what the puddles contain but also the sounds and sights that his investigations encompass: "As it began to get dark, the frog chorus spread and intensified into a syncopated din. Gray spectral shapes like giant owls flapped out of the dusk and landed in the fields—night herons that roosted all day in the willow thickets to the north. They were joined by several egrets, and the darkening fields became a mob scene of strutting gray and white birds that croaked and flew aside like melancholy ghosts when I walked past." For the trained observer like Wallace, the myriad life of the most unlikely places is there for the senses to perceive, and it is his special gift that enables the reader to share his perceptions.

Wallace is even more unusual in the scope of his interests. These essays range geographically from the Bay Area and northern California to the Alaskan wilderness, the Okefenokee Swamp, the Connecticut River south of Hartford, and a remote shrine high in the Japanese mountains. In subject matter they range from the tiniest of creatures to the large vertebrates, from the Scioto madtom to the pelican, the beaver, and the bear. Wallace is equally at home in, and fascinated by, sea-level swamps and estuaries and remote mountain meadows. Far more that most of us, he is at home in the world.

But being at home in the world does not mean that he is always comfortable in it. Wallace is, I think, in love with the planet we inhabit and with those who share it with us, but his love is unsentimental. It includes the recognition that nature is not benign or hostile; it is itself, obeying no human laws. It is therefore fully capable of producing phenomena that threaten human beings. Like any other creatures, as individuals and as species we are at risk. We are also, as Wallace makes plain, the source of menace to a natural order that is at once powerful and fragile. More than any other creature, we have succeeded in altering the natural world, and we have done so with insufficient attention to the effects of what we have done and are doing. Most obviously this is the case in the weaponry we have developed from the split atom, and in the depletion of energy sources produced by millions of years of geological activity. These essays make clear, however, that the obvious dangers are not the only ones. Wallace shows that the American landscape and most of its ecosystems have been altered irrevocably by what we have done to them, and that we simply do not have anything like enough knowledge to have any idea of the long-range effects of our tampering.

At the same time, Wallace is no Jeremiah threatening us with destruction. He specifically rejects the role of the nature-elegist who weeps literary tears for natural changes. In a thoughtful essay on those who write about nature, he reminds us that the idea that nature is a loser is a myth, once useful in the encouraging of the growth of civilization and knowledge. But it is only a myth: "Nature is not a loser because it is not a competitor." There is a sanity in these essays that rejects easy formulations, whether elegiac or sanguine.

This healthy sanity is an integral element in the personal quality that pervades all of David Wallace's writings. He never poses as the detached, objective observer. Without saying so, he is clearly aware of the scientific principle that the presence of an observer affects what is observed, so he never tries to remove himself artificially from the scenes he depicts. It is our good fortune that when he looks into the murky depths of Oakland's Lake Merritt or paddles through a Georgia swamp, he takes us with him and shares with us the sights and insights he finds along the way. We become confident that this friendly guide will show us the trees, the shrubs, the flowers, as well as the fish, the birds, the worms; we recognize that, in doing so, he will show us how each fits into the system of which it is a part. We can be grateful that the voice in which he does so will be gently ironic, open, amusing, never strident even when it conveys anger or fear or disgust.

The ability to achieve all of this is a function of the style of a marvelously skilled writer. David Wallace has found the means to convey, with an apparent simplicity that belies the hard work that has produced it, not only the facts of the worlds he examines and the responses they evoke, but the awe-inspiring sense in his readers that they are in the company of a skilled observer who is also a trustworthy and intelligent companion. As an interested but not detached student of writers and writing, I cannot tell you why this is so; I can only say that it works wonderfully well.

JOHN M. MUSTE

Taos, New Mexico
August 1986

# I  GROWING THINGS

# The Untamed Garden

SENSIBLE people take up gardening because they like fresh, inexpensive produce. That isn't why I took up gardening. I took it up because I had a vision of harmonious participation in the natural world. The vision came to me while I was driving a taxi on the night shift in San Francisco in 1970. My memory of the vision is a little hazy, actually, but it had something to do with ladybird beetles, and with the idea that living things are supported by other living things. It seems a laughably rudimentary idea, but it hadn't struck me before, at least not within the context of actually doing something about it. It suddenly seemed wonderful that people could live by growing vegetables and eating them, and that they could enlist the support of ladybird beetles, earthworms, soil bacteria, cows, and songbirds, not to mention the vegetables themselves, in doing so.

I moved to the country soon thereafter and took up gardening in a manner predictably incompetent: I threw some manure on the ground, churned it with a spade, threw seeds into it, and more or less abandoned it to an infestation of Bermuda grass. The ground I was trifling with wasn't my property, so not having to make mortgage payments on it, I was spared the more depressing implications of my incompetence. I found the tidal wave that broke over my plantings interesting. I had never noticed weeds to any great extent. There were so many different kinds: bindweeds like white morning glory; two varieties of curly dock, dark green and red; umbrella-leaved mallow; feathery mustard; spiky sow thistle—so many different ecological responses to the question of how my vegetable plot might be usurped. I had not realized nature was so ingenious.

I lived in a number of places during the next decade, which didn't improve my gardening skills. I'd rush out with a spade on a beautiful spring day, fling quantities of lettuce, pea, and radish seeds into soil that was deceptively dark and moist after its long winter's nap, and carefully protect the pretty seedlings for a few weeks. But as the soil got thinner and thirstier in the heat, and the plants larger and more demanding, I'd get tired or distracted. I never seemed to get much more than a meal's worth before the pea vines turned brown and the radishes and lettuces began to flower.

Perhaps I never would have risen above that stage if I hadn't married a woman who, after observing my peculiar behavior for a couple of summers, took a more practical approach. Betsy worked the soil enough so that the plants could get their roots into it, and she fertilized and watered it enough so that the roots could get something *out* of it, and we began to enjoy some excellent and bounteous produce. Betsy's success didn't encourage me to emulate her painstaking approach—I'm still mainly a digger, weeder, and seed-flinger who prefers using muscles to brains in gardening—but it did provide me with actual living gardens to ponder. My original vision of harmony has been somewhat modified as a result.

Gardening is participation in the natural world, all right, but it is about as harmonious as the Saturday nights in North Beach of my taxi-driving career, when hordes of tourists, prostitutes, dope-dealers, policemen, soldiers, sailors, and God knows what else (Saudi Arabian airline pilots, Olympic Peninsula dairy farmers, penniless black teenagers) surged in and out and about my cab as I careened over the steep cobblestones and cable-car tracks. In both enterprises, gardening and taxi driving, there's absolutely no way of knowing what will happen next. Vegetables are like taxi passengers in that one is never sure whether they will pay. A patch of weeds is more predictable than a garden. If one digs up a piece of ground, one can be certain that mallow, dock, bindweed, and sow thistle will grow on it, and that they will give way eventually (if the ground is not disturbed again) to grass, trees, or other permanent vegetation—what ecologists call "climax" vegetation. (Weeds are "pioneer" vegetation.) If one plants vegetables, the outcome is problematic. Most are unlikely to bear fruit without disturbing their sponsor's peace of mind in some way, and usually more than once.

From an ecological viewpoint, gardening is the essence of disturbance, a ramshackle pseudoecosystem that has evolved piecemeal from seeds and tubers in our prehistoric ancestors' garbage piles. Most garden plants not only thrive on but require constant disturbance. Of course, we call that disturbance by names like "care" and "cultivation," because its results care for and cultivate us, but anybody who has ever dug into the dirt and turned up a clod full of hysterical earthworms knows what he is doing to their little world. From a worm's-eye view, a garden must be a place of dizzying cataclysm and revolution, of ecological boom and bust, as mountains of rich compost and manure are abruptly crammed into the soil, then almost as abruptly sucked out of it by the roots of the monstrously overgrown plant mutants we call vegetables. To a worm, a garden must be a place of famine, drought, flood, earthquake, and pestilence, since it is not only fertilized, dug, and harvested, but fallowed, watered, and sprayed.

When I say constant disturbance, I mean *constant* disturbance. As a visionary gardener, I was much taken with the notion that one could "build" a fertile soil with compost, manure, and other estimable stuff. I got the idea that there would be some point at which the soil I was building would be finished, some point at which I could stop shoveling manure, lie back, and harvest crop after flourishing crop from my edifice of humus. I've been working on the same garden four summers now, however, and I haven't noticed any diminution of its appetite for organic material. Sometimes sitting on the lawn in the evening, I think I hear slurping and chewing sounds from the other side of the privet hedge. My raised beds sink and shrivel perceptibly through the long California summer, and by the end of the growing season, the soil is just about as powdery, pebbly, and gray as it was when I first dug the beds. (The soil isn't packed as hard as it was originally, which is an advantage of raised beds with the garden paths running between them. Even so, the sun bakes a pretty good crust on the top layers.)

My garden isn't conducive to notions of progressive evolution. It doesn't accumulate virtues the way I thought it might. That it produced nice lettuces and carrots last year is no necessary precondition to their production this year. My garden is unlike my bank in that it doesn't give interest. I'm the one who has to give interest. It's possible, of course, that I haven't been working long or hard enough to build a progressive soil. But how long did it take glaciers and tall grasses to build the prairie soils, and how long has it taken us to deplete them?

That isn't to say we have to start the whole garden over from scorched earth every spring. My wife planted some nice beds of perennial flowers and herbs (I look out the window and see clary sage and yarrow almost as tall as I am), and I (getting practical where my sweet tooth is involved) have maintained some serviceable berry vines. But I don't feel as confident about even the perennials as I might have a few years ago. Those clary sage plants must be using up an awful lot of soil fertility to get so tall. Something will probably have to be done about that.

Vegetables and annuals also regenerate themselves, albeit in unexpected ways. Last year, melons grew in the bean bed, tomatoes in the lettuce and spinach, cucumbers in the squash (giant, *orange* cucumbers). This year, huge borage and potato plants shot up in the paths (along with a mullein whose leaf rosette is up to my chest); and a gopher plant, a euphorbia we had planted sparingly the summer before to discourage its namesake, decided that a former pepper bed was paradise, covering it thickly. Certain plants, especially catnip, chamomile, calendulas, and dill, seem to grow just about anywhere, anytime. But despite my visions of natural harmony, all those self-seeding plants don't please me as much as they might be expected to. They seem too extraneous and untidy, which may reveal a self-serving side to my visions. I want the seeds *I* plant to thrive, not the ones that plant themselves. I want harmony on *my* terms. Fond hope.

My vision of gardening has been disappointed, as most visions are. It has been an interesting, amusing, and on the whole quite satisfactory disappointment, however. That not all the disappointments we experience in life are unpleasant is one of the great inducements to go on living. So it is with gardens. Somehow, the unexpected never quite disintegrates into universal chaos and destruction. Things sometimes even turn out better by chance than they might have as planned.

When we first planted the garden, we lost a number of tomato and pepper plants to pocket gophers, and I feared increased damage as the garden expanded. It hasn't happened; in fact, damage has decreased as the garden has gotten bigger. The only losses to gophers last year, when we had our largest garden yet, were two parsley plants and few carrots and potatoes. The gophers even ignored a large patch of beans, a vegetable I know they like because they had decimated a previous patch. It's not that there aren't gophers in the garden; their workings are all over the place. They just haven't eaten many vegetables.

I wonder, indeed, what the gophers *do* eat. Gardens contain mysteries as well as surprises. When we moved to this property, a fifth of an acre on the edge of a small town in a California mountain valley, it was piled with elderly lumber left by the elderly previous owner. Under those piles—and under the house too, this being a foundationless Depression cottage—lived numbers of large (presumably elderly) western toads. I find toads droll, and they eat insects. I looked forward to having plenty of toads in the garden, and during the first summer, I did. Toads popped out of gopher burrows or peered at me beady-eyed from under moonlit squash vines.

Toads have been less in evidence since then, however. I wonder if that is because of the disturbances I've caused on the property. I've turned the lumber piles into tomato stakes and stove kindling. Have I exiled my toads? Or have they simply found new hiding places on the property—places where I don't intrude, human blind spots where a toad can relax undisturbed? It's almost an epistemological question. Is there a toad reality contiguous to mine but immune to my inquiries? There *are* still toads; one startled me last night, rustling in the hedge. They are big toads. (Maybe they're dying of old age. I tried to import some little toads newly hatched from a nearby creek bed where thousands were hopping in all directions, like pebbles come to life, but they've become scarce, too. Big toads do eat little toads.)

I've tried to compensate for dismantling the lumber piles by building little dugouts around the garden edges. I don't know if the toads use them, though, because toads abandon hiding places if disturbed, and I don't want to drive them out of the dugouts by looking to see if they are in them. I envision them in there, packed cheek by jowl, corpulent from feasting on aphids, earwigs, squash bugs, weevils, cutworms, slugs, and cabbage moths, but I guess I'll never truly know if they're there. A dugout full of large toads might be an appalling sight, anyway.

It seems likely that I've somehow decimated my toad population by disturbing the habitat, which is another blow to visions of harmony. I'd have thought they would increase in numbers to take advantage of the burgeoning insect population my vegetables encourage. It didn't occur to me that they might resent, or at least not respond favorably to, being (quite inadvertently) shoveled into a wheelbarrow. I might console myself with the reflection that, if my disturbances have discouraged the toads, they may also have discouraged the gophers, but I'm afraid I'll never be sure.

Not all garden mysteries are so knotty. Some are satisfactorily solvable, though solving them doesn't necessarily promote harmony. Last summer, something started making large holes in ripe tomatoes and melons. Close examination revealed tooth marks. I couldn't think what animal might be making them. Deer never come closer to my property than the nearby creek bed. Jack rabbits and squirrels occasionally come hopping by, but I hadn't seen any recently. Coyotes or raccoons were possibilities, but the bites were being made night after night, with unlikely regularity for wild animals.

Eventually it dawned on me that a neighbor's cat had been spending a great deal of time in the garden, not just in the compost pile and freshly dug beds, which cats usually frequent, but in the tomato and melon beds. It was gratifying to solve the mystery and interesting to know that cats can be vegetarians. That knowledge didn't stop the cat. I can't think of any way short of electrified wire to keep it out of the garden.

I suppose my garden would be more predictable if I used electrified wire and other stern measures that would limit the antics of the animals and plants. Weeds are more predictable than vegetables because they are better adapted to the rigorous limits of the natural environment. But I've gotten to like the surprises and mysteries my unruly garden grows. I certainly don't like all of them. I don't like going out and finding that a whole bed of lettuce seedlings has vanished overnight. (Snails love perennial flower beds—best not to put vegetable seedlings next door.) I do like turning the sprinkler on a corn patch and seeing a flock of goldfinches descend to drink from the wet leaves. I like finding black swallowtail butterfly chrysalises on dill plants and wolf spiders sunning their eggs at the mouths of their tunnels under the tomato plants. I never get tired of the cleverness of the big black bees that frequent the nicotianas; unable to reach into the narrow corolla tubes, the bees get the nectar by piercing the trumpetlike flowers at the base. This spring, I especially liked looking out the window and seeing four black-headed grosbeaks, two western tanagers, a lazuli bunting, a golden-crowned sparrow, a white-crowned sparrow, a Wilson's warbler, a yellow-rumped warbler, two linnets, and a robin in the garden at once.

Most of the above creatures are benefiting the garden by eating insects or weed seeds, which is the kind of relationship that stimulated my vision of harmony. They aren't benefiting it enough to stop the weeds and insects, however. If they did, they wouldn't be around anymore, there being no insects or weed seeds left for them to eat. The harmony of songbirds in a garden is quite dependent on the disharmony of insects feeding on that garden, a disharmony that is dependent in its turn on the disturbance resulting from the garden's very establishment.

Harmony from disturbance? It doesn't seem sensible. It does, however, reflect what science has learned about the planet's workings in the past century or so. The day has passed when the

Earth could be regarded as an orderly hierarchy of creatures, as it was believed to be in the Middle Ages and Renaissance, or as a smoothly functioning machine, as the Enlightenment regarded it. Evolution has disclosed an Earth of incredible antiquity, which is neither orderly nor smoothly functioning, but has a kind of slapdash stability. Things get disturbed all the time—entire species and even orders of organisms become extinct—but a certain continuity is maintained.

A couple of billion years of organic evolution without a single instance of universal chaos and destruction seems a pretty good record. Continuity has been maintained not by perfect adjustments or organisms but by a continuing interplay of conflicting forces: of plant growth conflicting with animal hunger, of animal hunger conflicting with plant defenses, of plant defenses conflicting with animal teeth and mandibles. That dynamic equilibrium has existed throughout evolution and continues to exist throughout the planet, with no exceptions. Each gardener can hope and strive to reach an advantageous position in his plot's ever-changing equilibrium of plants and plant-eaters, but none of us should expect to be the only creature to benefit from the disturbances we initiate.

# Gardening with Pests

WHEN I set out to start a garden two springs ago on some land I'd just bought, I immediately had an encounter for which none of the organic-gardening books had prepared me. I was breaking ground with a spading fork when a small, reddish-furred creature suddenly appeared at my feet, baring its teeth, obviously upset. It was a pocket gopher, and it had good reason to be unhappy. I'd accidentally disemboweled it in its burrow with my spading fork.

I ended the gopher's suffering with a rock and felt a disquieting mixture of satisfaction and sadness. There was one less gopher to molest my vegetables. None of the gardeners I told about the encounter expressed the slightest sympathy for that gopher, rather envy at my luck in having dispatched it so easily. Still, it had seemed an interesting, beady-eyed little creature. It reminded me of some pleasant times I'd spent in wild areas, watching gophers busily pushing earth out of their burrows, or watching coyotes perform their almost balletic gopher-catching dance—first absolute stillness, then a rearing back on the hind legs, a quick pounce with the forepaws, and, if successful, a toss of the head to flip the stunned gopher out of its burrow.

The encounter brought up an aspect of gardening that is curiously absent from books about "natural gardening." The backyard plot that one wants to turn into a garden is usually occupied territory already, not as spectacularly occupied as a forest or prairie, but with wildlife populations that are just as dependent on it as the bison were on the virgin prairie. One doesn't usually associate today's backyard organic gardener with the hard-bitten types who broke the plains and killed the bison, but both disturb established ecosystems. There was a certain uncomfortable irony about my encounter with the gopher. I'm the kind of person who would like ranchers not to exterminate the coyotes, mountain lions, and eagles that might prey on their lambs; but here I was killing a gopher that might prey on my carrots.

Of course, there's no way to live in this world without killing—directly or indirectly. The gardener fears the gopher for the same reason the rancher fears the coyote: because it might kill something that he wants to kill or eat (or sell) himself. But it seems to me that there are two different approaches to the problem of relating to the original residents of a piece of land one wants to use. The first is to exercise maximum control, to raze the garden plot down to bare earth as completely as possible. My neighbors use that approach. Their garden is a brown rectangle from which every weed and pest is excised with almost surgical precision as soon as it raises its head. Their garden is also exceptionally productive, and I have great respect for them as gardeners, although I can't understand how they reconcile their total vegetarianism with killing gophers with poisoned peanuts. The other approach is to limit controls, to try—as much as possible—to fit the garden into the ecosystem that was there first. This approach by no means precludes killing weeds and pests when they become troublesome. It does imply a certain sensitivity to the lives of weeds and pests, a willingness to explore their possible benefits to the garden or the world at large, and an admiration for their often-fascinating life histories, connected as they are with those of more desirable garden plants and animals.

The second approach concerns me here. I see nothing wrong with making one's garden a superproducing vegetable machine (I do see a great deal wrong with attempts to turn the entire planet into a superproductive vegetable machine, but that's another matter). As a naturalist, though, I think that by taking such an approach one misses some interesting opportunities. Like most people in the United States, I don't get my entire living from a garden, so I don't begrudge myself some entertainment from gardening, along with the honest sweat, energy conservation, and free food. Even if I did make my whole living from gardening, I probably would still want to get some fun from it, and to me the antics of the other organisms with which I share my property are as amusing (if not always as tranquilizing) as television.

I probably got more entertainment than food from the first year of my present garden. The pocket gopher, for example, is one of the most marvelously adapted burrowers on the planet, a creature that people might pay money to see if it weren't in their backyards already, eating their string beans. The gopher is an integral, ineradicable complement to the soil in the drier parts of North America. Indeed, there is evidence that the gopher has to a considerable degree *made* the soil in those parts, performing the same function with its burrowings as the earthworm in moister climates. (I certainly didn't turn over many earthworms as I dug my California backyard—I think I found three.) Every year large expanses of the valley where I live are covered with an inch or two of soil the gophers have pushed out of their burrows. Since it seldom rains here in summer, and the soil gets baked quite hard, one can imagine how infertile it might become without gophers to break it up, aerate it, and fertilize it with their droppings.

It's difficult to think of a creature better designed to handle such an ecological task than the gopher. Built like a bulldozer, with shoulders and forepaws capable of pushing large heaps of dirt before it, the gopher has additional specializations that make a bulldozer seem primitive. Its lips close completely *behind* it's four front incisors, so that it can use them to sever roots or break hard ground without getting dirt in its mouth. As with other rodents, a gopher's incisors never get dull because they are always growing. It can use teeth and paws to burrow while carrying food or nesting material in the fur-lined pouches outside its cheeks (hence the "pocket" of its name). Of course, the gopher reproduces itself, something bulldozers have yet to do, and it does so with the help of a rather startling adaptation. Gophers have narrow pelvises, in keeping with their tunneling life. In fact, the female's's pelvis is too narrow for giving birth, so when she becomes pregnant, the pubic bones of her pelvis simply melt away, their elements resorbed by the body under the influence of ovarian hormones. The gopher matron spends the rest of her life without pubic bones.

Gophers use all that equipment to make tunnels so vast and intricate that early explorers on the Great Plains spoke with awe of sinking in perfectly dry but gopher-riddled soil, as though they were in a quagmire. "Gopher" derives from the French term for honeycomb, *gaufre de miel*. A single gopher's tunnel system may cover an acre, with a main tunnel five hundred feet long and a number of side tunnels leading to larders, privies, and nests. Mounds of soil pushed out of these tunnels have been known to be a foot high and ten feet across, although they're usually much smaller. In Washington State there are strange, hillocky areas suspected of being the work of exceptionally large or industrious prehistoric gophers.

Fortunately for gardeners, gophers do not pool their burrowing abilities. Except during mating, they are solitary creatures. Although burrows may get entangled, giving the impression of a colony, each animal keeps to its own tunnels, sealing off inadvertent penetrations into the tunnels of others, and ferociously attacking gopher intruders. The gopher's dislike of its own kind may be a reason not to kill one in a garden, if it's not being destructive. If it is removed, another gopher is likely to move in, perhaps a more destructive one than the first. I certainly didn't enjoy a gopher-free garden after accidentally spearing that first one. On the contrary, tomato, eggplant, and pepper plants quickly began to be mowed down by a gopher that may have been digging a new burrow. It didn't eat the plants, just severed the roots, as though they were in its way. Damage to tomatoes and peppers stopped later in the summer, perhaps indicating that construction of the main tunnel was complete.

That is not to say that gophers don't eat vegetables. They love the bean family, and my summer resident had a burrow entrance in every patch of bush beans in the garden—originally vigorous plants that the gopher gradually worried to dejected remnants of former glory. I did get a fair quantity of beans before the gopher became too enthusiastic about them, but I kept thinking, if only the stupid rodent had been a bit more forbearing—if instead of biting off the plant at the stalk it had just picked the beans—we could both have had more. The gopher did less damage to pole beans, which were out of its reach for the most part, so I planted more of these this summer, and spaced out bean-family members so that other plants don't get damaged in the gopher's rush for the beans. The gopher also did some insulting things to lettuces and flowers, but that was about the extent of its damage. Gophers are said to love the onion family, but a row of leeks has gone ignored for six months.

Gophers aren't the only burrowers on the property. There is also a mole, which seems to stay in the lawn and front flower bed. Moles do less damage in gardens than gophers because they eat mainly insects instead of plants. The mole tore up part of the lawn in early summer, perhaps during nest construction, but hasn't been noticeable since. I hope the mole stays. We have a lot of crane flies around here (crane flies look like giant mosquitoes), and their burrowing larvae can be destructive to lawns. Mole diggings are distinguished from gopher diggings fairly easily. Moles often burrow just below the surface, forming a ridge, whereas gophers never do. When moles push earth out of their burrows, they do so straight up, forming a conical mound. Gophers push earth out at an angle, leaving a more fan-shaped, untidy heap.

The other major burrow dwellers in my garden are completely beneficial, since they don't dig burrows, just live in them. In late spring my wife and I began to think we had Peeping Toms. Startling loud rustling sounds were coming from below our windows at night. We went out with a flashlight and found several of the biggest, fattest toads I'd ever seen, crawling out from under the house. They looked as large as dinner plates—like lumpy, flattened clods of earth that somehow had sprouted eyes and legs and started hopping around. The toads promptly moved into the gopher's burrow system in the garden, where, judging from their girth, they must have eaten thousands of earwigs, moths, beetles, and other nocturnal insects. I'd go out at night with a flashlight and see what appeared to be a pair of black eyes sparkling solemnly from the earth itself—as though my garden had grown sense organs—until I discerned the outline of the toad's body around the eyes, its warty hide having taken on the same flat, pebbly contours of the ground where it crouched at the entrance to a gopher tunnel.

Toads didn't turn up only at night. There was one gopher hole in a bean patch from which—when I watered the patch after sunset—would regularly emerge a dignified toad that I half expected to be carrying a towel and bar of soap, ready for its daily shower, although I suppose the real reason for its emergence was that it didn't like being flooded in its resting place. Another time, I dug up a stony patch in the garden to fill a hole in the driveway. When I poured a bucketful of this soil on the driveway, one of the "stones" bounced and squeaked indignantly, then waddled off and somehow inserted itself into an inch-wide crevice in a pile of boards—quite an astonishing feat, since the toad itself was at least six inches wide. It just flattened out and *flowed* between the boards.

It's surprising what a variety of creatures live under things on my property, which is only a fifth of an acre at the edge of a small town. Muffled creaking sounds from the bowels of gopher tunnels are the calls of the Pacific tree frog, a diminutive species that changes color like a chameleon. Depending on its surroundings, it may be green, brown, gray, or a tasteful combination of all three. Tree frogs are even better at getting into tight spots than toads. My wife once went to get some fabric from a box in the tool shed and found a mottled gray and green tree frog nestled among her batiks and paisleys, as though it had become fascinated with the problem of matching such challenging patterns. Tree frogs seemed to have a particular affinity for the lettuce patch, where they turned a contented-looking green and, I hope, ate plenty of slugs.

The garden also came equipped with large, sluggish alligator lizards; small, nimble fence lizards; and at least two species of snakes, although one of these can't truthfully be called a native because I imported it. Hoping it would live up to its name, I kidnapped a gopher snake that was inoffensively crossing a nearby stream bed and introduced it into one of the gopher holes. Gopher snakes are large, gentle (to humans) snakes that dig their way into gopher burrows and kill their prey by constriction. Unfortunately, I haven't seen the gopher snake since I released it, and I'm afraid it's gone off in search of better hunting.

The snake's apparent disappearance points up a major problem with biological pest-control by predators such as gopher snakes. I might get a gopher snake to eat the gophers in my garden, but then there would be no more gophers for it to eat, and it would leave. For predator-prey relationships to function, there must always be more prey than predators—which is fine for the predators, but troublesome for the gardener. The only way to get around that problem is to keep throwing disproportionately large numbers of predators at the prey so that no matter how many leave or starve to death, others fill the gaps in the ranks. That is possible with easily cultured, prolific insect predators, such as ladybird beetles or praying mantises, but difficult with gopher snakes or other vertebrate predators.

As a consequence, I don't have enough toads, frogs, lizards, and snakes to stop prolific invertebrate pests. Even a pair of robins that nested in a tree right beside the garden and spent every daylight hour relaying invertebrates from soil to nestlings didn't stop them. Actually, the robins seemed to take mostly centipedes—which prey on garden pests in their own rights—so the birds may have neutralized their control value somewhat by preying on another predator. Biological control can get tangled in some pretty complicated biology—but then, so can chemical control.

Invertebrate damage was not as dramatic as gopher damage, but much more sustained. Seedlings kept disappearing, abruptly or gradually, nibbled by earwigs, slugs, wood lice, and tiny leaf-miner larvae. Earwigs were particularly bad, apparently because the previous winter hadn't been cold enough to reduce their population. I probably could have reduced the earwig problem by putting out rolled-up newspapers as traps (they hide in them during the day, like vampires in coffins, and can thus be conveniently taken up and burned) and by removing compost and manure piles from the vicinity. Earwig and wood-louse populations reach astounding proportions in weathered manure; when I dug into an old pile left by the previous owner, I felt for an uncomfortable moment as though I'd been stricken with delirium tremens, so much fevered crawling was going on around my spade. There really wasn't anyplace else for the compost and manure to go, though, and by that time I was getting almost as interested in toads and earwigs as in vegetable seedlings.

Invertebrates are frustrating to deal with because they work so inconspicuously. One day, the seedlings are there; the next day they're gone. I suppose that is one reason people like to use chemicals on them—pesticides are even sneakier than insects.

At least one insect in my garden stood up and gave a fair fight, though. Tomato plants were infested with tobacco hornworms, which reached hot-dog size and thus allowed one to take vindictive satisfaction in their destruction. The leaf-patterned green caterpillars were hard to see as they chewed languorously on green tomatoes (although their sequin-sized, dark-green droppings under the plants were a giveaway), but once located they could easily be picked off and consigned to the compost—making me the direct agent of control, a satisfyingly simple ecological relationship. One doesn't necessarily have to *like* pests in order to be entertained by them.

Hornworms are fascinating caterpillars, if one doesn't mind caterpillars. They are named for wicked-looking spikes on their tails. When picked up, they rear back, make gnashing sounds, and wriggle as though trying to sink this "horn" into one's hand. I haven't been able to discover if that's just bluff or if the "horn" actually is a weapon, but I'm not about to stick myself with one to find out. Tobacco hornworms are the larvae of the Carolina sphinx moth, a rather beautiful moth with an orange-banded abdomen and intricately patterned, pearl-gray wings. It comes out in the evening to hover over flowers and sip their nectar with its long proboscis, rather as a hummingbird does. I don't mind losing a few tomatoes to have sphinx moths in my garden. Frost killed many more of my tomatoes than hornworms did, anyway.

Physical factors such as frost are much more of an obstacle to gardening than pests. It seemed as though tomatoes had just begun to ripen when cold September nights kept them green on the vine. And the poor fertility of the backyard soil was harder on vegetables in general than were gophers or earwigs. It was full of rocks, chunks of concrete, and rotten wood, with a whitish, alkaline quality, and I didn't have time to build it up with manure and compost before planting the first garden. Some things didn't grow, even though unmolested by pests. An okra patch was shunned by gophers and insects alike, but the pathetic little plants never grew more than six inches tall anyway. The few dozen okra pods they produced were bigger than they were, as though they were midgets pregnant with normal-sized children.

The poor soil did confer one advantage, though. Weeds seemed to find it even harder to grow in than did vegetables. The only weed that flourished was pigweed (*Amaranthus*), and I understand it's one of the more beneficial weeds for pumping nutrients from the subsoil to the surface. Where they weren't competing directly with vegetables, I let the pigweeds grow until they began to flower before pulling and composting them. That compost went into a winter bed that vigorously sprouted lettuce, spinach, radishes, and leeks, which we're still picking six months after planting. The only other weeds of note were a scattering of sow thistles, which also are reputed to be beneficial, and anyway were so frail and spindly that one could hardly imagine them troubling the big, hairy, smelly tomato plants. Despite the gopher tunnels under them, several of the tomato plants were bigger than I am.

This season, the soil has been improved enough to grow more weeds. After all, weeds are a minor problem as long as one has the time and inclination to pick or hoe them. I'm usually willing to do so because I almost always find interesting creatures in the process: velvet ants, which are wasps that look as though they're wearing peroxide wigs on their heads and abdomens to disguise themselves from the bees they parasitize; Jerusalem crickets, big predaceous burrowers that remind me of little men in suits of lacquered armor; diminutive brown mantises that run faster the hotter it gets, so that they seem to disappear in an animated blur as the temperature reaches the hundreds in the midafternoon.

I feel less sanguine about gophers than I do about weeds, though. That they didn't do excessive damage one year doesn't mean they won't another year. More intelligent than weeds and caterpillars, they are less predictable, less amenable to real or imagined human hegemony. What does one do when gophers become obstreperous? Trapping them in their burrows is said to be the most effective control method. I bet every hardware store within the gopher's geographical range carries gopher traps. A problem with this method is that one had better not mind trapping gophers because one probably will have to keep doing it. The gopher is one of those species—like the coyote—whose reproductive potential exceeds the traps' potential for reducing its population. I suppose there have been cases in which gophers were trapped out of gardens and never returned, but I doubt there have been many.

No amount of interest one might feel in the natural history of garden pests can completely insulate one against outrage at the damage they do. I remember breaking into a cold sweat on finding yet another wilted, tilting tomato plant that the gopher had wantonly bitten out of its path. At such times, I was ready to get out the traps. It's a little odd, when one thinks about it, that a gopher or caterpillar can generate so much emotional heat simply by eating a tomato or bean plant. If we lived in hand-to-mouth dependence on gardens, that would be reasonable, but most people probably lose more money to parking tickets every year than to gophers without seriously thinking of setting bear traps for meter maids.

Garden pests seem to generate feelings rather similar to those caused by human thieves and burglars—a sense of violation and a fear of being further victimized, which are sublimated into rage. People still do things to gophers and coyotes that they were doing to human criminals two hundred years ago—chopping them in bits, flaying them alive, hanging up the mangled carcasses as an example. I have little hope that such tactics will deter the pests—they didn't even deter the more imaginative human criminals, who at least were aware of the wrong they were doing and the punishments they faced. There's no evidence that garden pests have any such awareness.

Perhaps the anger people feel toward pests is a relic of an earlier time when the world was a more anthropomorphic place than it is now. It was only a few centuries ago that people thought common animals had thoughts, morals, even language. Animals were burned as witches or executed for other criminal offenses. It is easy to feel, when a gopher topples one's treasured tomato plant, that it does so maliciously, in the knowledge that the plant is not its own to topple. The scientific observations of past centuries don't support this, and most people today know it, but perhaps it will take another century or two before that knowledge sinks in emotionally, before people *feel* that garden pests simply are carrying on instinctive activities without ill intentions.

Maybe gardening will have less potential for heartbreak then. I doubt it will entail less hard work and exasperation in dealing with pests, no matter how innocent their depredations are perceived to be. The poor may not be always with us—I hope they aren't—but I suspect garden pests will be. Pests aren't outlaws; they are constituents of ecosystems that thrive in response to our manipulations of those ecosystems. As we continue to manipulate ecosystems, they will continue to respond favorably.

# The Dungheap

THE previous tenant of the house had been a whirlwind of energy, scattering piles of lumber, rolls of fencing wire, a solar collector, a washing machine, a wooden tower, a flatbed truck, and assorted smaller objects across the property as might a tornado that briefly touched down before roaring off into the distance. I wasn't too sanguine about these gifts, most of which were broken or of dubious utility, but I immediately warmed to a large pile of horse manure he had deposited beside the derelict outhouse. My new neighbor echoed my feelings after introductory pleasantries over the back fence.

"Whatisname said I could have the manure pile," he said.

"Um, we were looking forward to using that ourselves," I replied, feeling miserly and apologetic, but obdurate. I offered him the lumber, the solar collector, the wire, the tower, the truck, the washing machine . . . anything but the manure. He said he'd think about them.

The yard was thoroughly overgrown with weeds, but nowhere were they as lush and tall as on the manure. Wild oats as tall as my chest waved over it. I cut them down, and a few weeks later they'd grown back to waist level. It makes one envious of horses and other grazing animals, that their excrement requires only a few months of lying in sun and rain to grow them another generous meal. But there were no horses on the property, so I started a compost pile with the cut oats. They would have to rot for six months, then be applied to the soil and exploited by potato or cabbage roots before they could become human food, destined in its turn to nourish kelp and sea urchins after being flushed into a sewer.

All that was speculative, though: first the garden had to be dug and the manure put on it. My spading fork poked two inches into the soil and stopped. I dug around and eventually pulled a chunk of concrete about a yard square out of the ground, a chunk that turned out to be one of several. Garden archaeology. There were wormy boards, rusty nails, broken bottles, and an amorphous, malodorous object that made me wonder briefly if I'd wandered into an Alfred Hitchcock scenario. Nowhere was the soil too stony and hard-packed, however, not to support an unbroken carpet of tough, fibrous grass roots, the extracting of which was like pulling up an army of stubborn imps by the hair. They made a pile about the size of the dungheap. Under them I encountered perhaps a dozen scrawny, sluggish earthworms, all over a foot deep in the soil, as though hiding from the grim conditions at the surface.

When I finally got around to it, digging up the manure pile was refreshingly easy. The oat stems and their roots popped obligingly out, weighed down loosely with dark clods of dung. But it was also a little alarming: when I pulled up the first clod, I involuntarily jumped back in surprise. I had uncovered a mob scene, a dungheap metropolis. I don't think I've ever seen a greater density of animal life than under that square foot of horse dung—not in a tide pool, not in a slide under a microscope, not even in a swamp pool in spring. Evidently the interface of oat roots and horse manure is one of the richest habitats on the planet—representatives of most of the major orders of invertebrate life had flocked to it as might diplomats to an OPEC meeting.

The most numerous animals in the heap were a suitable shade of gray for diplomats, and scurried in circles just about as randomly. They also had appropriately armored hides for this age of terrorism, slightly resembling dimunitive tanks. They were oval, many-segmented creatures called pillbugs or woodlice, although they are neither bugs nor lice (both of which are insects) but crustaceans, land relatives of shrimp and crabs. Woodlice live in abundance under any moist log or board but not in as great abundance as in the manure pile. They covered every square centimeter of dung—all ages of them, from violet-carapaced youngsters the size of apple seeds to pearl gray, pumpkin-seed-sized adults.

Almost as numerous were reddish-brown earwigs, slender insects with pincer-like cerci protruding from their back ends, which they raised threateningly if I touched them. Earwigs get their common name from a medieval belief that they like to crawl into the ears of sleeping humans, perhaps to feed on their brains. They've been exonerated of this, but are still execrated because of a fondness for garden vegetables. I wasn't pleased to see them for this reason, or the hordes of snails and slugs that clustered in the oat stubble as though in expectation of boom times once the manure was applied to lettuce and tomatoes.

These crustaceans, insects, and mollusks comprised the grazing herds—the antelope and wildebeeste—of the manure habitat. Predators were less numerous, but more diverse as to species. Wiry centipedes snaked through the gray woodlouse horde like tongues of flame licking at charcoal briquettes. When I first lifted the manure clod, the centipedes were a brilliant purple-violet color, but they faded to duller reddish-brown after the hot sunlight touched them. Like some snakes, centipedes subdue their prey with poison fangs—I hoped they liked earwigs, although they seemed a little small to prey on the insects.

Grayish spiders with jaws especially adapted to cracking woodlouse shells stood motionless among the swarming crustaceans—like lions lazily watching a herd migration. A long-legged orb weaver spider sat aloof in its web stretched among the oat stems, uninterested in non-flying prey, but a stout red, black, and gray jumping spider seemed to watch the commotion attentively with shiny black eyes. It may have been as surprised at the sudden unearthing of the mob as I, since jumping spiders are daytime, surface-dwelling creatures.

Another spider, a big gray and white striped wolf spider, seemed to be having trouble making its way through the throngs of woodlice. When I looked at it closely, I saw that its abdomen was covered with tiny spiders—young that recently had hatched from the round, white egg case that female wolf spiders carry with them so conscientiously that, if deprived of her eggs, a female will often pick up a pebble or twig to carry about as a substitute.

Largest and most impressive of the predators were three or four Jerusalem crickets that towered like elephants above the other animals. Jerusalem crickets are yellow-and-brown wingless insects that seem to be encased in sets of oriental lacquered armor, so stout and glossy are their chittinous hides. With large heads and rounded bodies and legs, they are strangely anthropomorphic, like tiny, hunch-backed gnomes. Though predacious, they are quite gentle and timid with people—they fold up their legs and play dead, then scuttle away and dig themselves into the ground so energetically that they disappear in seconds. I have no idea how they got their common name, since they are native to California (unlike woodlice and earwigs) and have no relationship to the Middle East that I know of. Perhaps the name arises from their speed in digging, as though they were demonstrating an ability to burrow straight through to the other side of the planet.

The Jerusalem crickets weren't the only ones to disappear in seconds. The rapidity with which the entire manure fauna disappeared from sight after I uncovered it was almost as breathtaking as its abundance. The manure was a living mosaic one moment, then, with an acceleration that reminded me of water disappearing down a good clear drain, the creatures dived for cover. In the blink of an eye, the manure seemed devoid of life except for a few loitering spiders. Even the snails and slugs had made themselves scarce somehow. Each time I pulled up a clod, the same thing happened: a mob scene, then complete depopulation. As I dug up more and more of the pile, it began to seem mysterious. Where were the hordes going? It seemed there should have been less and less space to hide in as the pile dwindled, but when I had transferred the last manure clod to the garden beds, there remained no sign of woodlice, earwigs, snails, centipedes, or Jerusalem crickets. The dry, hard-packed earth under the pile seemed an unlikely refuge for the manure-fostered multitudes.

This invertebrate ability to fade away quickly and quietly as a resource dwindles, seemed one that fossil-fuel-swollen human populations might profitably emulate as that not altogether un-manure-like resource also dwindles. Unfortunately, I can't figure out how they did it. It's probable that many of them went onto the garden with spadefuls of manure, as the tattered aspect of my beans and eggplants would indicate. It seems unlikely that most of the manure fauna could have been airlifted onto the garden by my spade, though, since most showed a distinct preference for avoiding it.

It really was surprising how quickly everything seemed to adjust to my destruction of the manure pile's great bastion of organic wealth, which had stood since the previous autumn, time enough for several woodlouse and earwig empires to rise and fall. I saw no hordes of refugees fleeing the leveled pile, no piles of starved or slaughtered corpses. Maybe my eyes simply weren't sharp enough to discern the death throes of manuredom. I suppose someone watching the earth from outer space during the next few fateful centuries will see the same outlines of continents and oceans, the same patches of green, brown, white, and blue, and perhaps think that humans have adapted to the loss of their dungheap just as easily as earwigs and woodlice seemed to. Or maybe nature is more forgiving than we tend to think, and our petrofat will soak back into the planet without really spectacular suffering.

Anyway, my free dungheap is gone, swallowed with almost audible slurps by the hard-packed clay and pebbles of the garden, along with several bags of store-bought, sterilized steer manure, fifty pounds of lime, bone meal, wood ashes, and anything else that came to hand. The only remnants of its existence are a few blackish clods under the peppers and tomatoes, and even they are dwindling as relentless gophers plow up the ground and pull the tomato plants under. Which demonstrates, if anything, that though the future may not be horrid, it will not be boundlessly rich. One doesn't inherit a dungheap every day. If I were a woodlouse, I might prefer living in a garden to living in a dungheap anyway.

# The Fifth Season

This summer I moved back to the Bay Area after living in Ohio for several years. I was used to the intense green of Ohio summers, and looked at the brown grass here with something of the midwesterner's disapproval. You call this summer? At the same time, I was glad to see the yellow hills. During the five years I'd lived here before, I'd grown to like the spiky desiccation of California summers. They gave bite to an environment that might otherwise have been tediously benign.

The old complaint about California not having seasons is, of course, wrong. The dry season is California's winter, its plant dormancy period. For some reason, though, our culture doesn't really want to acknowledge the dry season. Millions of people swear by cold winters, and like nothing better than to put on down parkas and romp in the snow. Very few revel in cavorting through the chaparral and dry grass on a blazing California August day. The very idea seems perverse, although dry-grass cavorting is actually the more "natural" of the two pursuits according to generally held theories of human origins. A biped ape of the African savannah would certainly be happier in a California August than in an Ohio January. Perhaps modern humans are repelled by the dry hills because it reminds some forgotten corner of their brains of a time when they were leopards and baboons in the tall grass.

Californians tend to treat their dry summers as though they were embarrassing lapses of taste. They cover them up, sweep them under the rug. Cities are full of evergreen plantings and painstakingly watered lawns. For every garden of native grasses, chaparral plants, and oaks, there are thousands of artificial edens of hibiscus, banana trees, and tree ferns. Freeway borders are carefully, almost obsessively, planted with evergreens—eucalyptus, oleander, redwood, pine—anything to avoid showing the traveler a bare branch or a patch of dead grass. Somehow the barrenness of a snowscape is considered pretty, that of a dry landscape ugly.

I think we lose something important by covering up the dry season—the element of change. Change is the one universal attribute of life, and it is often very frightening; but attempts to avoid it usually turn out worse than letting it happen. The green and white California cities look a little like cemeteries during the dry season. There is a similar preoccupation with an eternal springtime. Like most easterners (I grew up in Connecticut), I was favorably impressed with eternal springtime when I first came to California in 1968, but I've since come to view it with suspicion. There's something embalmed about it. The wrinkled body of the old, unwatered California may be a little scary, but it is the true source of renewal here.

There are difficulties about coming to terms with the dry season and giving it an honored place beside the four traditional Anglo seasons. For all its harshness, the California dry season is actually quite fragile. It very quickly shows the marks of mistreatment or neglect. A golden meadow of dry grass and tarweeds turns into a dusty trash heap when subjected to any degree of trampling or littering. The native perennial grasses are beautiful plants perfectly adapted to living through dry summers, but they've been largely wiped out by livestock grazing and competition from introduced annual grasses. The native oak trees seem to be headed in the same direction, since the heavy grazing that goes on in most areas makes it difficult for them to reproduce.

Wildfire is a factor that makes it difficult to appreciate dry summers. California plants and animals are adapted to periodic fires—California suburbs, of course, aren't. It's all very well to have your dream home nestled in greenery until a wind from Nevada sends a conflagration crackling over the ridgetop. Then the homeowner may wish for a backyard of bare dirt, like the adobe pueblos of Spanish California.

I can think of one way to let a bit of the dry season back into California cities. Freeway borders might be good places for native perennial grasses, since they aren't grazed or trampled. In the Midwest, freeway borders are kept mainly in grass. The grass is brown and dead in winter, of course, but in spring it quickly comes alive with an array of wildflowers that keeps changing through the summer and early autumn. In April there are dandelions and clover; in May, daisies and birdsfoot trefoil; in June, Canada thistles, fleabane, and hawkweed; in July, milkweed and black-eyed susan; in August, sunflowers and ironweed; in September, asters and goldenrods.

If California freeway borders were kept in grass, a progression of wildflower bloomings would be conspicuous from February through July. Some "unimproved" borders have become seeded naturally with lupines and other native flowers, and I find these much more attractive than the exhausted-looking ice plant and English ivy so dear to the hearts of highway department landscape architects. The native flowers change. They remind us—as we zoom along on our asphalt errands—that the planet is alive.

I can imagine the highway department's objections to my freeway planting plan: it would foster weeds; it would increase fire danger; it would put horticulture crews out of business. Roadside evergreens are also said to buffer noise and air pollution from freeways, but this seems a bit like putting a Band-Aid on a chain saw cut. Nobody really expects a row of eucalyptus or redwood to protect humans unfortunate enough to live beside an eight-lane freeway.

To return to the above three objections, then: seeding freeway borders with grass might allow some weeds to become established, but grasses tend to out-compete the worst agricultural weeds, which need plowed ground to sprout. The eucalyptus and oleander plantations also have their share of sow thistles when they haven't been herbicided recently. Dry grass in sum-

mer would increase fire danger somewhat, but it could be
mowed. In North Dakota they harvest hay crops from freeway
borders. Horticulture crews freed from planting and maintaining evergreens could carry out fire prevention projects, perhaps
including some controlled burns when air pollution wasn't too
bad. Wildflower crops tend to be best after a fire. Horticulture
crews could also plant and maintain a few native oaks. The
valley oak—the largest California oak—is probably in more
danger of extinction than the redwood.

I don't really expect the highway department to start planting
bunch grass and valley oaks. It must be cheaper and more efficient to plant the exotics and evergreens. Oaks don't thrive in
polluted air. Still, there are obvious limits to the artificialization,
the "greening" of the California landscape. We can't water the
entire state, unless we figure out a way to jack it up and drag it
north to the Olympic Peninsula.

Mediterranean climates such as California's have always had a
tricky, almost perfidious relationship with civilization. With
their gentleness and fertility, they seem to offer an unbounded
stage for realizing the human potential, but the fragile dry season also offers a spacious arena for human destructiveness and
carelessness. The sunny California of the American optimist
keeps flopping over into some burning vision of hell. Newspapers talk about the "dark side of the California dream," but this
is mere convention—violent people like sunlight as much as anybody else. The hot winds of the dry season were legally recognized as extenuating circumstances in murder trials of early
California.

Much of ancient history can be read in the light of this Mediterranean schizophrenia. From Mesopotamia to Italy and North
Africa, huge urban empires grew rapidly through use of aqueducts and irrigation, then collapsed just as rapidly in a welter of
social and ecological disasters related to the semi-arid climate—
soil salinization and erosion, drought and resultant famines, destruction of irrigation systems and aqueducts by invaders.

It's no accident that John Fowles's latest novel *Daniel Martin*
begins in Los Angeles and ends in the vast, completely deserted
city of Palmyra in Syria. Parallels between ancient Roman and

Californian civilization are obvious, particularly to someone in a green, stable culture such as England's. To a nature lover, there's a deep satisfaction in imagining Los Angeles completely deserted, but other aspects of California's going the way of the ancient civilizations would be less agreeable. The mountains would be completely deforested, for one thing. It would be better if we could figure out some way to make friends with the dry season.

The first step in this direction will be a semantic one, since all things human begin with words. We will have to invent a name for the dry season. It's ridiculous to call it by the same name as the growing season of the temperate deciduous forest. Perhaps we could use a name from one of the California Indian languages. They must have had a number of very suitable ones.

Once the dry season had a name, we could proceed to institutionalize it. There would be dry season holidays—people could hang decorations on leafless California buckeyes (a tree that loses its leaves in July). There would be a dry season art—sentimental chromos of little tin-roofed shacks nestled in the blue oaks and manzanita. There would be dry season sports. I'll leave the imagining of them to the reader.

# The Way of All Grass

ONE of the few places I know in the Bay Area that may resemble the original native grasslands of California is a little hillside behind the East Bay Regional Park District office near the intersection of Skyline Boulevard and Redwood Road in Oakland. The east-facing hill looks like any other grassy slope from a distance—green in winter and spring, brown in summer and fall—but a closer look reveals something quite different from the wild oats, mustards, and thistles that cover most California hills today. This slope is covered with native bunch grasses and wildflowers, with a greater diversity of species than is usual. Every time I go there, it seems, I find new plants.

One of the most rewarding visits was in the middle of last June. The hillside was studded with brilliant yellow mariposa tulips, lily family flowers that are aptly described by the double reference to tulips and butterflies in their name. Usually found in relatively undisturbed grasslands, mariposa tulips are a rare sight in the Bay Area today. Even more abundant than the tulips on the hillside were lacy, white-flowered tarweeds, sunflower family plants that get their name from a sticky secretion on their leaves and stems that protects them from desiccation during the dry season. And almost as numerous as the wildflowers were red, black, and white butterflies called chalcedon checkerspots, which were clustered so thickly on some plants that I thought at first they were huge, showy blossoms.

Many wildflowers that had peaked earlier in the spring were still in bloom. There were California poppies, lupines, blue-flowered Brodeias (which resemble elegant ornamental candelabra), bright pink Clarkias. I found many seed pods of blue-eyed grass, a small relative of iris that had covered almost every square foot of the hillside in April and May. At that time large patches had also been covered with goldfields, another small relative of the sunflower.

I wasn't able to identify any species of grasses on that visit. Most had already passed their flowering stage, and the only way to definitely identify most grasses is to dissect the florets and key them out according to small details in structure. It's the kind of nature study that could make you blind or insane. But even without definite identifications, it was obvious that there were many more species of grasses than wildflowers on the hillside. There were big, droopy grasses with flowering stems up to my chest, medium-sized grasses with tidy, pale green bunches of basal leaves; small, spiky grasses growing among rocks on the drier areas of the hillside. Botanists employed by the Regional Park District have identified about fifteen native grass species on the hillside (which is only a few acres in extent), including purple needlegrass, pine bluegrass, fescue, brome, barley, melic, and bentgrass.

Botanists think the native grasses and wildflowers have persisted on the hillside because its soil is formed from serpentine bedrock. Serpentine is poor in the nutrients needed by the aggressive annual weeds that have taken over most California grassland, so native plants already growing on the serpentine have been able to resist the encroachment of the alien annuals. The apparently tranquil hillside is a kind of botanical Indian reservation—a shrunken tribe of natives making a last stand on a piece of ground that the invading enemy has been unable to exploit.

The plights of California Indians and native grasslands have been curiously parallel. Both were thriving, stable, and admirably adapted to their environment when the first Spanish explorers arrived. Both were reduced in less than a century to scattered survivors in places unwanted by the invaders. These decimations are probably among the greatest ecological catastrophes of all time, and they raise a troublesome ecological question. If the Indians and native grasses were so well adapted to their environment, then why was it so easy for invaders to replace them? How could organisms that had been evolving here for hundreds or thousands of generations be swept aside almost immediately by organisms that had evolved halfway around the world? This seems to contradict the idea, fundamental to the environmental movement, that survival depends on ecological harmony.

This question is more easily answered in the case of the Indians than the grasslands. To oversimplify somewhat, the native cultures were swept aside because the invading Europeans rapidly destroyed the environment to which the Indians had adapted, replacing it with another environment to which the invaders were adapted. Wheat fields and cattle range replaced the valley savannahs with their elk and antelope herds. To some extent, the same thing happened to the native grasses where they were plowed up and replaced by crops and orchards. But there are also huge areas of the state where native grasses were never plowed up, but were replaced by wild oats and thistles anyway.

Drought and livestock grazing probably played a part in this replacement, but botanists don't seem to think they were completely or even largely responsible for the demise of native grasslands. They seem to think that the annual weeds are simply more efficient at growing and reproducing in California than the native perennials. The fact that land removed from grazing or any other disturbance fails as often as not to revert to native perennial grassland seems evidence of this. It's a matter of "survival of the fittest," although there seems to be no clear idea as to exactly why annual weeds are fitter than native perennials.

Evolutionary thought has gone beyond the identification of "fitter" with "better," however, and it is perhaps a little early to close the book on native California grasslands, even though they are so decimated that the Nature Conservancy has been unable to find even a few acres that might be called "virgin." For one thing, the native grasses have been swept aside so abruptly that they have hardly had a chance to show their value as livestock and wildlife food, as ground cover, or simply as part of a healthy, stable ecosystem. Some obscure native grass might even have the potential to become an important food crop for humans. An obscure native grass recently discovered in the Mexican mountains turns out to be a perennial relative of maize, offering potential for cornfields that would not have to be plowed up and replanted every year, with considerable lowering in rate of oil depletion, soil erosion, and human labor wherever corn is grown.

Even if native bunch grasses don't turn out to have any dramatic usefulness, I think they should be perpetuated for their beauty, interest, and diversity. I get tired of hillside after hillside covered with wild oats, star thistles, and filaree. Not that these Old World plants don't have a beauty of their own, but I think they lack the diversity and subtlety that the native perennials have evolved during their millions of years in this part of the world. The annuals are like Forty-Niners—vigorous and colorful, but lacking a certain grace and quiet nobility that the natives display.

Ever since the 1930s drought, there has been a movement in the Midwest to restore and preserve some of the native tallgrass prairie, which had been almost as badly decimated by agriculture and overgrazing as the California bunch grasslands. Today almost every regional park agency in the Midwest has its restored or preserved prairie area. Even the agency I worked for in Ohio (not exactly a "big sky" state) has one. Prairies are restored by burning and plowing the weeds and brush off a likely field, then seeding the area with prairie perennials such as big bluestem, Indian grass, blazing star, rattlesnake master, and compass plant. Once established, the prairie is burned over again every few years to keep weeds and brush from reinvading. Prairie fires were probably the major factor maintaining the virgin tallgrass prairie—many parts of the Midwest that were once "seas of grass" are now heavily wooded because fires were stopped.

I'm not aware of any corresponding native grassland restoration movement in California, supposedly such an environmentally progressive state. The grass on the hillside behind the Regional Park District office wasn't restored—it persisted on its own. Bunch grass restoration might be less feasible than tallgrass prairie restoration, since we aren't sure why annual weeds have overrun the native perennials so completely. To burn a hillside and seed it to native bunch grasses and wildflowers might not work. I don't know if the experiment has been tried. If it has and been proved futile, there might be other ways of restoring some of the native grassland. It would be nice if each regional park had its little plot of needle grass and mariposa tulips to delight the eye in June, when the wild oats and mustards are dead and brown.

# II FIELD NOTES

# Puddles

COYOTE Hills Regional Park, near Fremont, California, is a good place for one of my favorite winter sports—splashing around in puddles. No equipment is required, except perhaps a pair of rubber boots. The only requirement is an expanse of flat, poorly drained, wildish land on which to splash, trying not to sink in above the knees and generally getting muddied, warmed by the winter sun, and ventilated by the breeze. The object of the sport is to absorb some of the extraordinary vitality that arises from the ground as it is replenished by the winter rains.

On one visit last winter, I parked at the entrance and started toward the Ohlone Indian mounds, walking around or through large grassy puddles that covered most of the trail. A willow-bordered slough ejected various startled marsh birds as I came abreast of them—an American egret, a small flock of cinnamon teal, a black-crowned night heron, a pair of mallards. A white-tailed kite (a beautiful white and black hawk that hovers like a kite on a string while watching for frogs and insects to pounce on) sat on a fence post across the slough. A marsh hawk skimmed over the water, throwing some coots and a pied-billed grebe into a momentary, splashing panic.

At the mounds the trail stopped being a string of puddles and became a small river, so I had to turn back. I idled in the sun a while and took a closer look at the puddles. What had appeared at first glance to be sterile expanses of muck and submerged grass turned out to be teeming with rapidly revolving greenish specks—probably one of the many species of crustaceans (water fleas or copepods) that inhabit puddles. These creatures had evidently spent the dry season as eggs in the soil, hatching out in incredible numbers when the rains came. Here and there a larger red speck could be seen pursuing or clutching one of the greenish specks. This was an aquatic mite, a tiny relative of spiders.

Much less numerous than the specks, fortunately, were mosquito larvae, also called "wrigglers" because of the way they move through the water by undulating their cylindrical bodies. There were also many small creatures—probably some species of water bug or beetle—that swam so energetically and hid so effectively that I couldn't see them well enough to definitely identify them. Every puddle I examined had a complete supply of revolving crustaceans, predatory mites, undulating nascent mosquitoes, and hyperactive beetlebugs. The spectacle reminded me of those animated cartoons on intergalactic monster wars featured on Saturday morning television.

While peering into these mini-galaxies, I kept being startled by male pheasants that flew over my head with a great squawking and flapping. In ten minutes three pheasants flew over, landed in a nearby field, and sneaked away into the weeds. South Bay flatlands probably are (or were) among the most productive pheasant habitats in the world. Then a strange racket began coming from a patch of cattails—a squeaky bubbling sound with angry overtones. The racket was so loud and emphatic that I was surprised when the small brown bird that made it finally hopped into view. It was a long-billed marsh wren, a bird that lives only in marshes and so is not a common sight in these days of channelization and drainage canals. The wren eyed me, let out another string of wren curses, and flew into another patch of marsh vegetation, startling from it a yellowthroat—a bright yellow warbler with a black mask across its eyes.

Prevented from going beyond the Ohlone mound by the deep puddles, I went back to the entrance road and walked south across more semiflooded land that had evidently been in crops before the park was established. It was better drained than the land near the mounds—there weren't any willow-bordered sloughs—but there was still plenty of life. A lone egret stood meditatively in a weed patch perhaps looking for a snack of meadow mice, flocks of kildeers flew over making sounds of lament, and Pacific treefrogs became increasingly vociferous in ditches and wet spots as the sun declined. I almost stepped on a pheasant in one patch of burdock and sow thistles. A field in the distance was a grazing and foraging place for a half-dozen California ground squirrels, a pair of black-tailed jackrabbits, and a motley crowd of shorebirds—sandpipers, willets, and avocets. The black and white avocet plumage was very bright against the emerald and gold of new grass and flowering mustard.

As it began to get dark, the frog chorus spread and intensified into a syncopated din. Gray spectral shapes like giant owls flapped out of the dusk and landed in the fields—night herons that roosted all day in the willow thickets to the north. They were joined by several egrets, and the darkening fields became a mob scene of strutting gray and white birds that croaked and flew aside like melancholy ghosts as I walked past. I had all these flatland spectacles almost entirely to myself. There were plenty of people in the park, but they stayed on the hills or on the boardwalk that ran across an all-year marsh west of the mounds. The weedy, puddled fields weren't an attraction, which shows something about American attitudes toward landscape. It was a little strange to see all those people swarming across the unspectacular little Coyote Hills with the vast Diablo range looming in the background. Why bother climbing Coyote Hills when the Diablos are nearby?

If our aesthetic of landscape was based on rarity, the flatlands around Coyote Hills would be the most treasured landscape in the East Bay, since they are part of a very small remnant of flatland not yet covered by warehouses, factories, or tracts. But flat land that doesn't at least have a thick marsh on it hardly seems to exist as landscape for Americans, regardless of its rarity in a natural state. I'm not sure if this disdain for flat land arises from the wholesale uglification we've perpetrated on it, or if the uglification is a result of the disdain. I tend to feel that the former is more true, that the conversion of valley land to heavily poisoned factory farms, smoggy industrial wastelands, or fantasy suburbs has closed the option of appreciating valley land for Americans in general and Californians in particular. One has only to glance at a few nineteenth-century landscape paintings to know that those people took as much pleasure in flat countryside as in hills or marshes—definitely more in the case of marshes, those being the days when malaria was still prevalent in California.

It's a little frightening that a whole area of landscape appreciation—probably the oldest area since hills and wetlands were not seen as conventionally beautiful until the Romantics began extolling them in the late eighteenth century—should have been erased from the American psyche in less than a century. "Growth" evidently covers more than land with suburbs and freeways—it also seems to cover large areas of the human spirit.

I learned to love flatlands by moving to central Ohio, where one had better love flatlands if one is going to love any land at all. One warm day in March, while walking through a swampy woodland near where I worked, I idly began peering into the rivulets of snowmelt that meandered across the path. I began to see surprising things. Twigs and clots of sand crawled across the bottom. They were caddisfly larvae, which cement tubes of sand, muck, or leaves with a sticky secretion and live in them like snails in their shells. Grayish-white specks swam about in the water and kept changing shape—from thin to fat, and back to thin again. I scooped up some of the gray specks and saw that they were planarians, the droll, arrow-shaped flatworms featured in every biology textbook. Wild planararians! For some reason this greatly impressed me. It was like finding a dinosaur in the backyard. Life is stranger than biology textbooks.

The rivulets were like tide pools; the more I looked, the more I found. There were hundreds of red spider mites, orange horsehair worms like coils of copper wire, inch-long fairy shrimps so brightly colored they might have escaped from someone's tropical aquarium. There were aquatic insects of every kind—backswimmers, water boatmen, striders, whirligig beetles, giant water bugs, predatory water beetles. In sunny, grassy places, brown or green chorus frogs the size of large grasshoppers inflated bright orange throat sacs and made sounds reminiscent of thumbnails being drawn across the tines of large metal combs. My ears rang for about twelve hours after listening to these tiny frogs close up for perhaps fifteen minutes.

And it wasn't even a real swamp! It dried up completely in May. The real central Ohio swamps—the few that were left—were even more impressive. Wood frogs, spring peepers, and toads added their voices to the chorus of frogs; seven-inch-long spotted salamanders crept over the bottom like baby alligators; and two-foot snapping turtles slept gargoyle-like on fallen logs.

The Coyote Hills puddles seem tame and dull compared with those Ohio puddles. I don't know if this is because the California puddle fauna is inherently poorer than in the Midwest, or if it's because the Coyote Hills flatlands were cabbage fields until recently. I know there are some very interesting California puddle flora and fauna such as that of vernal pools. Once you get past the poetic name, vernal pools are puddles that leave successive rings of unique wildflower species as they dry up in the spring. Vernal pools are hard to find in California today, though, and I've never had the chance to examine one. Perhaps the Coyote Hills puddles would develop into something more characteristic and interesting if left alone long enough for a diverse flora and fauna to become reestablished, although it's hard to say just what the native flora and fauna might have been, aside from the willows and treefrogs that survive.

I phoned the East Bay Regional Park District to ask about the past and future of the Coyote Hills flatlands, but I didn't learn much except that the area is under the jurisdiction of the Alameda County Flood Control Board and that the duck marsh will be enlarged as part of a flood control plan. I asked if native vegetation would be reestablished on any of the flatlands, but the idea didn't seem to interest the planner I talked to. The field where I watched night herons flying out of the dusk will be a parking lot and picnic area.

# Of Pelicans and Pantyhose

LAKE MERRITT, in Oakland, is said to be the oldest wildlife refuge in the United States, having been set aside in the mid-nineteenth century as a preserve for migratory birds. It is certainly one of the most unusual. It is man-made, to begin with, having originated when Samuel Merritt dammed a tidal salt marsh to make a more imposing setting for the towns and mansions that were going up in the vicinity. Lake Merritt's present location in the middle of one of the most strenuously urbanized areas in the country also sets it apart from most wildlife refuges, which tend to be in fairly pristine places. Perhaps most unusual—or at least most surprising—is the often extravagant quantities of wild organisms that the lake engenders and supports, despite its super-civilized location and artificiality.

As I write this, the first winter storms are passing through, bringing two phenomena to Lake Merritt that epitomize its peculiarity. First, the many storm drains that empty into the lake have washed an entire summer's accumulation of litter, grime, and spilled crankcase oil into the lake, an incredible welter of plastic, paper, dead cats, torn underwear—anything imaginable—all filmed with an iridescent oil slick that curls and swirls on the lake's surface like an old-fashioned psychedelic light show. At the same time, the storms have brought large flocks of migratory and/or marine birds to the lake, where they will spend much of the winter sheltering and feeding. It would be tedious to list all the bird species that winter on Lake Merritt—there are so many of them—but they include ducks, grebes, phalaropes, gulls, pelicans, terns, coots, egrets, and cormorants. What do they feed on among all this muck and garbage? Unbeknown to the joggers that huff and puff around it like uncoupled choo-choo trains, Lake Merritt is a rich, functioning ecosystem (although I wouldn't venture to say whether it is healthy).

A few minutes of looking into the lake water reveals the basic elements of this ecosystem. Mingled with the flotsam of Styrofoam cups and Big Mac containers are filmy strands and sheets of algae, the photosynthetic producers at the base of the lake's food pyramid. During the warm summer months, tremendous blooms of algae fill the lake, causing disagreeable, sulphurous smells, but also fostering large populations of small shrimp and other tiny invertebrates. These populations serve in their turn as food for small fish—mainly smelt and gobies—which breed enthusiastically and reach astronomical numbers by summer's end. A long glance into any shoreline stretch of the lake at this time will often reveal schools of smelt that shadow every inch of lake bottom with their nervously darting bodies. Algae, small animals, and bacteria also serve as food for substantial numbers of clams, mussels, and interesting aquatic worms that live in white, limy cases and filter food from the water with dark-green, bushy gills. Most of the lake bottom is covered with a melange of mollusk shells and worm cases left by deceased residents, while living clams, mussels, and worms live hidden in the muck or attached to the stone walls around the lake (or to beer cans, scrap metal, or other convenient substrates).

In the fall lowered temperatures and chemical changes in the water kill most of the algal bloom, which causes something like mass panic and famine among the swollen animal populations of the lake. Driven by this environmental stress, huge numbers of small fish come into shallow waters, pursued by the larger fish that feed on them, where both become vulnerable to the newly arriving migratory birds. Sometimes entire schools of fish die off all at once, attracting vociferous flocks of gulls, which, lacking the fishing skills of cormorants, egrets, and diving ducks, usually have to fish from the sidelines or steal larger fish from the other birds.

Lake Merritt's odd combination of urbanity and biological productivity makes it about the best place to watch fishing birds close-up that I know of. The birds are used to humans (especially joggers—I've seen joggers run past a line of egrets and gulls without causing a flicker of movement in the birds although they all fly away when I walk past) so one can often watch them stalking or catching fish from a few feet away. (A little circumspection is required, however; the birds are quick to become nervous and flee if stared at or directly approached.)

This past fall the assemblage of birds was spectacular. A flock of brown pelicans had been feeding in the inlet between Kaiser Center and Lakeside Park, perhaps a dozen adults and half again as many brown-headed juveniles (which is an encouraging sign given the decimation of pelicans by DDT in the 1960s). The pelicans would sit on the water with their improbable beaks tucked down against their breasts, then somehow get a signal that a school of fish was nearby and take off with an ungainly flapping that turned abruptly into graceful soaring just above the water's surface. When they spotted fish, they would dive into the water and open their bill pouches so that they seemed to have veined, water-filled balloons attached to their chests. I suppose a number of small, schooling fish can be trapped in a single such maneuver, to be swallowed when the beak pouch is deflated and raised out of the water, as indicated by gulping movements in the pelican's throat.

Actually, I'm not sure that the pelicans locate the fish schools—they are merely the most conspicuous members of the assemblage that prey on the smelt and gobies. The graceful little Bonaparte's gulls and Forster's terns would seem more likely fish-finders than the pelicans, since they fly higher and more nimbly, diving from ten or twenty feet to catch fish in their sharp beaks. I saw a Bonaparte's gull dive into about a foot of water directly below where I was standing on the sidewalk and fly away with a several-inch-long goby I hadn't noticed. Or maybe the cormorants with their underwater swimming abilities are the fish-finders that the other birds follow.

Whatever its origin, there is a definite coordination in the feeding activity of these various birds. When the pelicans, Bonaparte's gulls, and terns leave one part of the inlet and move to another, the snowy and common egrets and California and ring-billed gulls that have been lined up at the water's edge or in the shallows hoping for an opportunity to grab fish stirred up by their more efficient brethren soon follow, as a crowd of spectators in tennis whites might follow a game of water polo from one end of a swimming pool to another. Water polo is not such a farfetched analogy either—the splashing, shrieking, croaking, and belching of the birds would do justice to the most inebriated country club crowd.

Fall is the most active time on the lake. Large rafts of ducks stay on the sheltered east side all winter, but they don't make quite such a spectacle as the other birds, spending most of their time bobbing up and down on the water with their bills tucked sleepily under their wings. Often the log boom that separates the east side from the main part of the lake is completely covered with resting cormorants, like a receiving line of dark-suited, long-nosed gentlemen, stretching from one side of the lake to the other. Striped bass and small sharks are said to come into the lake from the bay when the flood gates are opened to let storm water out, though I'd never seen any.

In the spring most of the birds leave to breed in more secluded, salubrious spots (there are some little wooded islands offshore from the Rotary Nature Center in Lakeside Park, but a colony of black-crowned night herons that roosts there apparently makes short work of any duck eggs that get laid thereabouts). The water clears and becomes less littered after the rains end and before the algal bloom gets into full swing. This is a good time to look at the lake's underwater goings on, which are as interesting as the birds' fishing, if less obvious. Last spring I was walking along the lakeshore on a bright, warm day when I noticed small fish darting individually among the clots of algae that were beginning to form. They weren't smelt or gobies, so I stopped to take a closer look and saw that some of them were a bright, metallic blue color, with jewel-like red bellies. These bright blue fish hovered over certain algae patches and chased away other fish that approached. Sometimes they made quivering motions over their algae patches, or burrowed into them.

I realized that these were male sticklebacks defending nest territories. Sticklebacks are fish about which you read a great deal because of their curious breeding habits, but I'd never actually seen them before, and certainly hadn't expected to see them in downtown Oakland. As I proceeded along the shore, I saw that there was a male stickleback guarding an algae patch about every few feet—a stickleback metropolis. The males were building nests in the algae patches by burrowing tunnels into them. When the nest is finished, the male stickleback lures cruising, egg-swollen females into it by doing a zigzag courtship dance. Once in the nest, the female is encouraged to lay her eggs there by nudging motions from the male; then she leaves as the male enters the tunnel and fertilizes the eggs. The male then chases the thinned-out female away, repairs the nest, and again starts exhibiting his charms to suitably fat females until he has a satisfactory egg collection. He incubates the eggs by standing on his head in front of the nest and fanning oxygenated water into the tunnel with his pectoral fins. When the eggs hatch, he anxiously guards the tiny fish, shepherding them into a tight school. If a baby stickleback wanders away, the male darts after it, catches it in his mouth, and carefully spits it back into the main school.

I wasn't able to watch this entire process, since I would have been knocked down and trampled by joggers and roller skaters many times over if I'd tried, but I was able to pass that way again several times and observe the progress of the stickleback nests. By the first day of summer, the circular clots of algae were teeming with thousands of tiny fish, the upcoming stickleback generation, well-protected from predators in their algal blanket. One stickleback school happened to be hovering over an open copy of Basic Math that some joyous or despairing high-school student had evidently flung into the lake; and it was easy to imagine the tiny fish dutifully doing their additions and subtractions, perhaps instructed by a small, whitish-gray crab that was sidling over the mussel shells on which the upturned textbook rested.

# Life in the Cemetery

For sheer volume of plant and animal life, a large cemetery near my house probably matches any place in the Bay Area. It is tended enough to keep all the ornamental plants healthy, but not too much to stop a colorful mob of native and exotic weeds from rioting on the premises. Many of these plants are good food sources for various animals, and the cemetery might be compared to one of those gourmet delicatessens that feature edibles from all over the world. A hummingbird, for example, can choose from a wide selection that includes eucalyptus flowers from Australia and fuchsias from South America as well as the native flowers. In winter there seems to be an Anna's hummingbird singing squeakily from every eucalyptus tree. In spring Allen's hummingbirds arrive from Mexico and perform dizzying seesaw courtship dances in the shrubbery.

The abundance of good things in the cemetery, of course, occasions some competition. Hummingbirds are pugnacious little beings, given to kamikaze-style dive-bombing of intruders in their territories. There is something very impressive about a three-inch bird thus defending a hundred-foot eucalyptus, and the hummingbirds seldom lack targets for their proprietary wrath. Big flocks of cedar waxwings, robins, lesser goldfinches, and mourning doves descend on the cemetery in winter to gorge on pyracantha berries, liquidambar seeds, and other attractions.

Hummingbirds aren't the only bad neighbors. A general pushing and shoving goes on continually. Flocking birds play endless games of one-upmanship, the commonest form of which occurs when an aggressive bird flies directly at another and thus displaces it at its perch or worm patch. The displaced bird then usually goes and displaces another, less aggressive individual, and so on. Doves and quail—supposedly so peaceable—are particularly given to this sort of behavior.

Neighborhood squabbles are also endemic in the cemetery's mammal population. I often witness them when I sit in the tall grass of a steep hill behind the burial plots. Once I was startled when a field mouse suddenly tumbled squeaking out of a hole right at my feet. It had been forcibly ejected by another mouse, which then stuck its head out of the hole and eyed me for a long moment as though considering whether to give *me* the bum's rush as well. Another time the grass was alive with tiny, grayish shrews (probably a species charmingly called the ornate shrew) that would appear, chase each other back and forth, and disappear, in a manner highly reminiscent of silent screen slapstick.

Even the invertebrates are frenetic. I once watched several male wolf spiders competing for a female's attention on a fallen tombstone. Male spiders are skinny, dwarfish creatures compared with females, but compensate for their ectomorphism with their energy. These male wolf spiders acted like hyperactive teenagers at a dance, running in circles and jumping up and down on each other. Every once in a while, the stout female would emerge from her boudoir under the tombstone, and one of the males would rush up to her and wave his pedipalps (the spider's copulatory organ) in her face, thus inhibiting her from eating him. The nuptial pair would then zip under the stone together, slapstick and ribaldry combined. The female would emerge to choose another suitor a few minutes later, but I can't recall seeing any of the lucky males again.

All this turbulence is presided over dispassionately by the hawks that are the apex of the cemetery's food pyramid—a pair of red tails and a pair of kestrels. They are only too happy to take advantage of a moment of unwariness on the part of mouse or bird—an unwariness often resulting from too close attention to the joys of intraspecific competition. It is common to see a neatly removed quail skin beside one of the tree-lined drives, or a kestrel administrating the coup de grace to a mouse while perched atop a mausoleum. Not that the predators are any more neighborly than the others. The kestrels fiercely resent the red tailed hawks, especially at nesting time, and spend a good deal of time shrieking "killy! killy! killy!" and diving at the larger birds' tails as they soar over the hill. Only the scrub jays and Steller's jays seem to waste comparatively little time squabbling among themselves, as though they preferred to keep their intelligent, inquisitive eyes on the main chance instead.

It is easy to ignore this squabbling, and to experience the cemetery as a quiet, dignified retreat, which indeed it is. Given a choice, I'd rather live in a cemetery than in many places people inhabit today; the neighbors won't play their stereos loud enough to make the walls vibrate. Still, the riot of animals and plants in a place of "eternal repose" evokes some odd thoughts about the expectations people bring to cemeteries. A handsome marble monument in my local cemetery sums up one of the more common expectations with its epitaph: "Earth itself is not the goal, but stepping stone for Man." The large gopher population has undermined this particular monument so that one corner has sunk under the grass, causing a rather precarious tilt (some monuments have toppled or sunk right out of sight because of gopher burrowings). Depending on one's point of view, this expressly upward mobile but actually sinking monument could be either an emblem of earthly transience and the vanity of material things, or of the impossibility of disentangling the human dream from its biotic roots. When you start thinking along these lines, the cemetery becomes crowded with ambiguous emblems. They begin to squabble in the mind as energetically as the birds do in the trees.

A quail perched on a tombstone—a common sight—is one example. Birds are frequent symbols of the immortal soul, so this might seem a living emblem of resurrection, at least until the quail starts clucking in trepidation at one's approach and unloads a spray of birdlime on the granite before taking flight. Even more angelic than quail are the flocks of mourning doves as they fly over the landscape of green lawn, neoclassical tombs, marble columns, live oaks, and cypresses. In the westering sunlight of late afternoon, the dove-flocked cemetery might be heaven itself, although this impression is dispelled somewhat when the doves land and start gobbling weed seeds, the males (if the time of year is right) puffing out their breast feathers and strutting after the females in pursuit of ecstasy. The fluttering copulation of birds is a fairly ethereal sight, but not much used in religious imagery.

My favorite emblem is a large, circular marble fountain that overlooks the cemetery. It is one of these wedding cake fountains, with small basins on an ornate pillar that drip water into a large basin below. When I first saw the fountain, the small basin had become a mini-marsh of cattails, sedges, and other aquatic plants whose wind-carried seeds had evidently colonized it. The fountain looked a little like a Greek god wearing an Indian feather headdress because of these plants. The large basin was full of green algae and killifish, minnows that live on mosquito larvae. The minnows may have gotten there as eggs on the feet of birds that come to drink or bathe in the fountain.

I liked this peculiar little ecosystem, so I was disappointed to visit it once and find that it had been drained and the basins cleaned of mud and weeds. When I returned a few weeks later, though, I found that the water had been turned back on and the cattails and algae had grown back as though they'd never been removed. I didn't see any killifish, but the large basin contained something that seemed even more marvelous. Aquatic snails with golden, spiral shells were swimming upside-down at the water's surface, evidently feeding on floating diatoms. They swam by undulating the muscular "foot" on which terrestrial snails ooze along. Used in this way, the foot resembled a slightly amorphous pair of wings.

What an emblem of resurrection that was—creatures symbolic of a slow, earthbound existence flying through sunlit water in a basin that had been dry and lifeless only weeks before. It was like something out of the later T. S. Eliot. At the same time, the floating, sunlit snails made the transcience of life seem not at all unattractive. Why ask more of the universe than a little time of floating and feeding between the mud and the sky? The snails seemed to take eternity in their stride (or lack of it). We humans worry often about the shortness of our lives, but I think it is the *length* of them that really troubles us.

Whatever the viewpoint, I think all would agree that cemeteries are for the living more than the dead. They are a measure of wealth for one thing—of the ability to idle valuable real estate for sentiment. The sentiment may be misguided—ideally we would put the dead in the high-rise barracks along the freeways and reserve the quiet, tree-lined spaces for the living—but then the living demand so much more space than the dead. The cemetery's better than no quiet spaces at all. When I walk in it, I feel that the dead are generous proprietors of the trees and birds; that the unbulldozed life around me is a gift from them. In a very real biological sense, this is quite true.

# A Walk on the Ridgelands

IT is a steady climb to move southward along the ridge. The top narrows as we ascend, and the digger pines and goldencup oaks crowd around the dirt road. There are fewer signs of cattle here, more of wildlife. The road is laced with the quotation marks of deer hooves and wolf pads of coyotes. Flickers, jays, and acorn woodpeckers call loudly in the trees, although we can't see the birds. The day is overcast, and the ridgetop is above the clouds—objects are only fitfully visible as the clouds stream past. Sometimes they blot out everything except the dirt at our feet; sometimes we get glimpses of distant ridges. Once we walk past a patch of snow from a storm earlier in the month.

Suddenly there is a coyote on a little knoll in front of us. It is the same gray as the cloud-dimmed grass, and we only see it because it moves. It is small and shortlegged. As it runs into the mist, two taller, rangier coyotes materialize and hurry after it. A female and two males? This is coyote mating season. Their paws make no sound, and when they are gone, it is as if they had never been there.

We turn eastward and begin to descend the ridge. The slope is dark with bay, live oak, and madrone; loud with falling water. It drops steeply to the canyon bottom, where a creek runs high and soapy brown with silt. A few small sycamores grow among tumbled boulders of a rich blue color, like lapis lazuli. Their hues brightened by the rain, the boulders make a startling harmony with the cream and olive of sycamore bark. Upstream, a gigantic boulder covered with moss and maidenhair fern looms above the creek like a castle on the Rhine. The creekbed sand is marked by raccoon tracks.

We cross the creek and start up the east slope of the canyon. It is much gentler than the west, rising in a series of terraces that are covered with valley oak savannah—a parklike expanse of valley oak, live oak, and digger pine stately and regal enough to grace an English country estate. Some of the oaks are giants, and there is a lone madrone that might win a tree beauty contest for the grace and symmetry of its crown. A faint yellow haze of buttercups sets off the deep green of the grass beneath the trees. It is a beautiful place, but a little strange to us. We aren't used to such decorum in wild country. The landscape seems tended even though there is no sign of human activity. The grassy woodland seems to have as much of the arboretum as the wilderness in it, as though spirits kept it pruned, weeded, and mowed.

Then we become aware of at least one factor influencing the landscape. A red-tailed hawk lands in an oak and eyes a colony of ground squirrels—a rocky outcropping where the grass is veined with well-worn paths between burrow entrances. The seed- and grass-eating squirrels probably contribute a great deal to the mowed and weeded aspect of the savannah. They aren't in evidence today though; they don't like the wet weather. The hawk remains in the oak just the same as we move off.

Higher up the east slope, the gentle terraces run into winding ravines hung with bay and live oak. We pass one of the abandoned homesteads that dot this region. There are bed frames, chairs, a stove, a sink. There is an old white-enamel dipper such as cowboys drink from in Westerns. The homestead buildings have no walls, however, having evidently burned down at some point leaving all these furnishings open to the sky but unvandalized because people never come here. The beds and chairs must have been sitting thus unoccupied for a great many years, judging from their old-fashioned style.

Stands of Coulter pines grow at the heads of the ravines. Straighter and bushier than the digger pines, they give a Sierra feeling to a landscape in which vivacious little streams meander through miniature valleys where frost stays on the grass much of the morning. As we walk up one such valley, a bobcat bounds away up a pine-covered slope. It is small and slender with dark-banded legs and back. Its white tail patch shows through the trees for a moment after the rest of it has disappeared into the shadows.

The valley leads up to the ridgetop, where we emerge on a narrow plateau covered with a healthy little blue and black oak woodland. Trees of all ages grow in an open stand on light, gravelly clay worked by gophers to a springy consistency. A smooth lawn of grasses, lupines, poppies, buttercups, larkspur, and other wildflowers covers the soil, although most aren't in bloom yet. The black oak buds are just beginning to swell and show color, and their last season's fallen leaves—large, yellow, and spiny-lobed—contrast handsomely with the smaller, purlish-blue oak leaves that litter the grass.

If the valley oak savannah in the canyon is like an arboretum, this blue oak woodland is like a well-tended orchard of small nut trees—filberts or walnuts. It is a place of muted but rich colors and diminutive but harmonious shapes. There is a feeling of delicate vitality here, a feeling that usually characterizes places where well-developed native vegetation is relatively undisturbed. There is nothing grandiose about it, but it is a little like being present at the beginning of the world—edenic—although it will be much less so during the dry season.

The oak woodland seems a welcoming place also because we feel the first sunshine after a day and a night of rain. Then a huge gulf opens in the mist that has surrounded us, and the ridgetop becomes a vantage point overlooking perhaps a hundred square miles that—with the exception of some dirt road scars and a power line—show no sign of human occupancy. There is only a tangle of peaks, ridges, and canyons—some densely wooded, some grassy, some with a dark green dusting of chaparral overlying bare red volcanic rock.

We turn north again, following the ridgetop away from the hundred-square-mile wilderness that was just revealed. After a few miles, signs of cattle grazing begin to increase. There are fewer trees, more annual alien grasses such as wild oats. The bays and live oaks on the slopes show a definite browse line, as though someone had taken hedge clippers to their branches below four feet from the ground. Then we encounter a cattle herd, but these are not placid Herefords or Black Angus steers. They are rangy, motley beasts with functional-looking horns. They don't panic and lumber clumsily away as would Herefords; they stand and stare. We give them a wide berth. They may be wild descendants of some homesteader's herd.

The ridgetop begins to drop away, and we see another bobcat ambling along a lateral ridge about a half-mile below. We watch it with binoculars for perhaps fifteen minutes. First it goes up to a large oak and puts its forepaws on the trunk as though getting ready to climb it, then changes its mind. It stands still a moment, as though watching something, then lies down and starts to clean itself as if it were an oversized tomcat, twitching its tail back and forth with pleasure. The sun has emerged from the clouds again, and there is a temporary warmth. It is a much heavier cat than the one in the pine woods, and its body is not banded but plain gray, with a golden tinge around the head. Suddenly it jumps up and stalks something in the grass for several paces, then relaxes and sits a moment, and finally trots out of sight in a gully.

The country described above isn't in a national forest wilderness area—it's a dozen miles from Livermore, California, and about eight miles from San Jose. East Bay residents don't always think of themselves as living in a mountain range, but they do. It is the Diablo Range, and it stretches from the Carquinez Strait in the north to Pacheco Pass in the south, encompassing over 1,300 square miles of open space, much of it virtual wilderness. The Diablo Range has such scenic quality and natural diversity (from redwood forest on its west side to semi-desert chaparral and grassland on its east side) that it might very well be a national park or wilderness area if it wasn't the backdrop for a major urban conglomeration.

Instead, millions of people drive past the Diablo Range on their way to camp or backpack in the Sierras or the Big Sur area. I had spent four years in California, much of it in the Bay Area, before I became aware how much outstanding wild country lies within an hour's drive of the megalopolis. There is a good reason for this, of course: most of the area is private land. I have nothing against private land, but it does seem irrational for so many people to use so much gasoline to do things at least some of which could be done closer to home.

For some years there has been a movement to establish a national recreation area in the Diablo Range. San Francisco and Los Angeles both have national recreation areas in nearby wild country, and it seems only just that the east and south bay area should have one too. The area would not be established by wholesale acquisition of land as with national parks, but by a variety of measures to keep land in its natural state, measures such as acquisition of development rights and easements for public access. This would allow ranchers to go on working their land, at the same time letting hikers, horse people, and other recreationists use it. Recently the East Bay Ridgelands National Recreation Area idea got a boost when Congressman Phillip Burton included funding for a study of it in his Omnibus Parks Bill, passed in 1978. That study is now being conducted by the National Parks Services.

# A Dunk in the Eel

BEING attacked by a school of minnows is a curious experience. It tickles, which can be enjoyable or annoying according to one's mood. Like all expert ticklers, minnows go for the toes, although I don't suppose they intend to inflict torment; and they nibble at other exposed parts of the body as well. The bites of even the largest—three or four inches long—don't even begin to break the skin. Apparently, what the minnows are after is the film of dead cells that constantly sloughs off the human epidermis. Their enthusiasm for humanity does not extend to blood and muscle as with the South American piranhas. Still, it does take one aback to instantly be surrounded by hungry admirers upon lowering one's sweaty mammalian bulk into the minimally cool water of the Eel River's middle fork in summer.

The minnows are like mosquitoes. Swarms of them seem to materialize out of nowhere, probably attracted by the dissolving essence of humanity in the water. When swatted, they flee in panic for perhaps a foot, then turn around without a moment's hesitation and return to the feast. Unlike mosquitoes, they're just about impossible to hit or catch—they move too fast. But minnows aren't really as annoying as mosquitoes, so one feels less vindictive toward them. They don't produce the irritating whine of mosquitoes, at least not to human ears; although I suppose if we had gills and lived underwater, minnows might prove to be just as noisy.

I have no idea how minnows discovered that sunbaked human rind is delicious and nutritious, but it seems an interesting example of animal learning. Humans have not been dunking themselves in the Middle Eel for very long by evolutionary standards, so it shows quite a bit of ingenuity for a small fish. Maybe the minnows started by nibbling other animals—bears or deer that entered the river to catch salmon or drink (although the tiny fish would have to sort through a great deal of hair to reach a bear's hide). Indians lived along the Eel for several thousand years at least, and apparently were very conscientious about bathing, so it's possible the minnows picked up their anthropophagous habits from them. I wonder if the minnows discern a taste difference between this original fare and the suntan-oiled skin they nibble today.

There's certainly a lot of it to nibble. The heat and dryness of the Middle Eel canyon drive people inexorably into the water, and one passes a different group of inner-tubers, scuba divers, skinny-dippers, campers, or housewives reading bestsellers on their beach towels with each bend of the river—it's like a string of mini-Rivieras. In a landscape of small, tormented oaks and parched, prickly grass, the river seems a miracle of comfort, even when the sand on its banks is too hot to touch. One almost expects the water to dissolve in a cloud of super-heated steam, like a mirage.

But the man-eating minnows are there to prove that the river is real and permanent. I think they belong to a species called the speckled dace, a name that perhaps is misleading since dace are usually identified by the dark stripes that run along their sides. While they were nibbling me, I noticed that the minnows had bright, metallic speckles on their backs, so perhaps that's what the name refers to. When almost two dozen of them clustered around my feet and legs, I began to get an inkling of what a worm on a hook must experience. Being eaten by an animal while you're trying to observe it does not promote scientific detachment. Finally I couldn't stand it any more and crawled out on a rock. The dace hung around for a few moments until my smell had dissipated from the water, then headed upstream where my wife was swimming. When I heard her begin to giggle and thrash around, I knew they'd reached her.

A different school of fish emerged furtively from under my rock and began to eat clumps of filamentous algae as though they were cotton candy. These were suckers, named for the protrusible mouthparts that they use to vacuum food from the river bottom. With big, round eyes and placid, timid habits, suckers remind me of cows. They are the grazing livestock of a river, a staple food for otters and other predators of large fish, since salmon and steelheads are scarce in warm, slack summer waters. Most of the suckers in this school were small, but a few were fair-sized—nine inches or more.

A yellow-striped garter snake came swimming across the pool with its head protruding from the water, and I dropped into the water and swam along behind it. It isn't often that one gets a snake's-eye view of things. The snake swam to the rock for support while it considered my uninvited companionship, then dived suddenly out of sight. Snakes are always doing double takes like this—they really are very unwary, innocent creatures despite their insidious reputation. The human-snake antipathy is basically one of mutual panic. I was afraid the lunchtime crowd would be back if I stayed in the pool, so I let the current carry me downstream into some rapids (which one would only want to do in the summer in the Eel, since high-water rapids, common during the winter and spring, are not for swimming). It was like lying in a kind of conveyor belt jacuzzi. The river slid me lazily over boulders, lodged me temporarily under small, bubbling waterfalls, floated me across sunlit, pebbly shallows where small trout darted away from my shadow, and finally deposited me on a sedge-grown sandbar, where two things I'd never seen before were happening at once.

A bee was buzzing around my head, but it was a bee with large, pale-green eyes and a black and white-banded abdomen—not your usual honeybee or bumblebee. It landed on the sand, and, almost faster than my eye could follow, dug itself straight down out of sight, leaving only a small dimple in the quartz grains. Just before it disappeared, I thought I saw something dangling from its back legs. I thought perhaps it was one of those wasps (bees and wasps are in the same insect order) that catch spiders, paralyze them with their sting, and bury them to serve as a living food for their young when they hatch from the eggs laid on the spider's body. If you take apart the mud nests that dauber wasps build under eaves (it's preferable to do this after the wasps have departed), you will often find translucent husks of spiders, their soft parts eaten by the wasp larvae. The green-eyed bee or wasp didn't emerge from its sand tunnel, though, so I couldn't tell what it was doing. Several others buzzed around, but they only scratched at the sand indecisively and had no spiders in tow.

Then my attention was captured by a dozen or so damselflies having group sex on a leaning sedge stem. Damselflies are slender relatives of dragonflies (they hold their wings parallel to their bodies when at rest instead of perpendicular as with dragonflies) and come in a similar range of iridescent colors. The ones on the sedge stem belonged to a common species of which males are blue and females grayish brown—I could see that their activity was heterosexual if not puritanical. The embrace of the damselfly is about as far from the missionary position as one can imagine. The male clasps the female's neck with the rear end of his needle-like abdomen so that he's in front of her, and the two go about thus in tandem for extended periods. I've read several descriptions of how the propagation of the species is accomplished meanwhile, but they never seem to quite sink in, and might be too complicated to describe here even if I could remember them.

Anyway, the damselflies on the sedge stem were all embraced in this fashion, gentlemen before ladies, and they made a graceful pattern of arc shapes along the stem, like a string of cut-paper silhouettes. It was an odd sight. When I first focused on it, I thought it was a strange plant, but this illusion was dispelled when two males that happened to be facing each other reared up on their respective partner's necks (prothorax would be the correct term instead of neck, actually) and began sparring at one another with their tiny forelegs. For some reason the damselflies reminded me of an R. Crumb cartoon. I could visualize letter balloons above the insects' heads containing various rude expletives and vulgar ejaculations, and I wouldn't have been surprised to see tiny fedoras on the males' heads and 1950s flowered hats on the females'. Maybe they seemed ludicrous because, every few minutes, a breeze came up and drove the stem partway underwater. Although this inundation didn't seem to bother the damselflies, it seemed farcical to me, as though the participants in a porno film extravaganza were to be abruptly dunked in San Francisco Bay.

I don't know why the damselflies were behaving in a way that would interest Gay Talese. I've seen damselflies mating often, but not en masse, and not in such interesting and artistically contrived configurations. Many insects mate in swarms to make it easier for the sexes to find each other, but from the numbers of individually mating pairs of damselflies one encounters, this doesn't seem to be a problem with them. Perhaps they are natural voyeurs, just like people. They certainly weren't crowded onto the sedge stem for lack of space: they have the whole length of the Eel to mate along, a river that has been known, during winter floods, to carry more water than the Mississippi.

Of course, if southern California developers have their way, neither damselflies, minnows, nor skinny-dippers will have the whole Eel River anymore, since most of it will flow south through the Peripheral Canal to fill swimming pools and irrigation ditches around Los Angeles and San Diego. The stretch of river I've described might already be under forty feet of water if the Dos Rios dam had been built as first proposed, and it still may be built. The bottom of a reservoir is a peculiarly lifeless place, populated largely if at all by wormlike larvae of tiny flies, and with minimal light, warmth, and oxygen—not the kind of place where one would want to spend a vacation. On the other hand, it's not the kind of place where one would have to put up with man-eating minnows or lewd and lascivious damselflies.

# Lost Worlds of the Connecticut

WHEN I was growing up in Hartford, Connecticut, I invented a game. A tiny drainage ditch that was hidden on both sides by hedges and fences formed a line of demarcation between the backyards of my block. I pretended that this ditch, which ran during wet weather, was really a hidden river like the lost jungle rivers that I knew about from watching Tarzan movies on television. Since each backyard was landscaped differently, I was able to follow my river through a variety of natural regions, as though I was exploring a continent. From a gently sloping prairie graced with birches and dandelions, I would trek off across a flat steppe of sparse, dry grass; then plunge suddenly into a rain forest of ferns and mountain laurel that had been created by some careful, old lady gardeners. From there the going got rough as I fought through a tropical bush of honeysuckle vines growing over the back of a garage to emerge at last into a littered pine-barren that was usually the extent of my exploration, since the kids that lived there liked to throw rocks.

When I was too big to frequent backyards, I found another secret stream. It ran through a swampy woodland near my school and disappeared, beneath the houses that were going up everywhere, into a huge concrete pipe. The pipe held considerable fascination for us, and I remember wading far enough into it to be in complete darkness except for a golden coin of daylight in the distance. The woodland had been a farm once. Ram-shackle wooden bridges crossed the stream, and the remains of a mill and dam lingered near the pipe mouth. On June mornings, when the water was very clear, I watched catfish as long as my arm comb the gravel under the bridges. Big snapping turtles overgrown with somber moss crept among the rippling weeds, and there were many caved-in muskrat dens along the bank. The birds were exciting: bitterns, green herons, red-winged black-birds, and a cock pheasant flying past the white limbs of long-dead oak. Early one morning I saw a pair of wood ducks flying soundlessly upstream. Or I may have imagined that I saw them.

When I started driving in high school, I became aware that every part of town had its hidden waterway. If it was small, it was buried in a pipe. The larger streams ran behind dikes, con-crete walls, and nearly impenetrable second-growth vegetation. They were collectively called "Trout Brook," no matter what part of the suburb they ran through. I think the only ones that had any real knowledge of the truncated watershed were the mal-lards, which once startled me by flushing from a place where I hadn't even known there was water. Occasionally, like a ne-glected and resentful Dragon spirit, Trout Brook rose and drowned a park or a street for a little while, its opaque waters flowing under the elms like a polished pavement. But this hap-pened less frequently as more of the stream was engineered into passivity. Cow pastures upstream through which the waters had meandered were bulldozed into shallow, muddy puddles—flood control reservoirs.

Later I moved to Hartford, where an unassuming stream called the Hog River crept a few hundred feet past the apart-ment building where I lived and then (of its own accord, so far as I knew) dived underground. It surfaced briefly as a pond on the State Capitol Building grounds, then returned to oblivion. This pond was so hugely overpopulated with languid carp that I was sure they must have arrived at some kind of self-perpetuating, cannibal ecosystem. There literally seemed to be more carp in the pond than water. The other city fauna I en-countered were equally desperate. The rat colony in the sand-bank across the railroad cutting from my building lived under periodic BB-gun strafing from my fellow tenants, who didn't have much else to do on the long summer evenings. Late one February night, while I was waiting for a bus at the center of the downtown area, a terrified muskrat crept along the gutter past me. I followed him until he disappeared into an underground parking lot of the Travellers Insurance Company.

It wasn't until the last summer I spent in Hartford that I became acquainted with the greatest of the forgotten streams, the one all the others were seeking through their devious courses. I was hired as a deckhand on a Connecticut River tour boat, probably the first commercial boat of any size (65 feet) other than oil tankers and coal barges to use the river in fifty years. Every day we ran halfway to Middletown and back, a good twenty miles, but I rarely saw a living soul on its bank; just levees, bridges, power plants, factories, high-tension cables, sewage plants, dredgers, and the freeways that had been routed through the old waterfront districts, torn down ten years before. The only habitation I remember was a shack that some old World War I veterans used as a clubhouse. It got to be eery, as if human activity had so accelerated as to be finally and literally invisible from the slower vantage of the river, monolithic structures and a kind of mechanical disturbance in the air being all that remained to the naked eye.

This desolation was strange because the river was beautiful. Even as it flowed past the junkyards at the edge of town or the rank silty farmlands farther downstream, the big trees and the play of sunlight and sky on the water made it look thoroughly Romantic. In a few places, the natural flood meadows persisted, lingering microcosms of purity. They were flooded in early spring so that the yellow catkins of the willows stood out against the dark green water. It was a warming, aqueous world—like a dream. When the waters receded, Queen Ann's lace and orange day lilies smothered the ground, and hundreds of fireflies lit the evening mists that rose from the river. In the fall the water at the meadows' edges cleared to a bright, hard blue. The fallen willow leaves were like knife blades against it.

At twilight the river became extravagantly picturesque, as though it had studied landscape painting with Thomas Cole.

Placidly it reflected the rose and incandescent orange of the sunset while its oaks and elms faded richly into azure and purple. Swallows skimmed glassy furrows in it and flung themselves back above the treetops with perfect grace. As we passed the sandcliffs they nested in, the violet-green birds seemed as numerous as the swarms of rising gnats they pursued. The public remained largely unattracted by these charms, however, and the only way the company made any money was by taking out charter parties at night. This was risky because the boat ran aground or got stuck in the fog overnight fairly regularly, and the parties usually incubated some kind of drama before the run was finished—drunkenness, philandering, brawls, or injury being the commonest. The midnight river swept silently along beneath this turmoil; only the channel beacons relieved its darkness. You had to steer with a careful eye on the bank so that the dancers on the top deck wouldn't be whisked into the water by overhanging boughs. But the captain, a former executive whose psychiatrist had prescribed a more relaxed occupation, remained optimistic. He liked to tell the passengers that the river water would be drinkable by 1970.

I finally escaped from the world of suppressed waterways by riding down to the Connecticut's mouth in a friend's motorboat one Sunday. Houses began to appear on the bank as we passed from sandstone lowlands into a range of basaltic hills below Middletown. They were old houses, but they looked cared for and lived in. Gulls blew in our wake, and egrets and great blue herons stood on the bars and snags. Then the hills faded in the distance as we approached Long Island Sound, and the river spread out. Things dwindled between sky and water. Trees, boats, and houses became scattered flaws in the smooth expanse, like specks on a mirror.

We passed far below a bridge that seemed as tenuous as a spiderweb, and the estuary opened out. The river finally seemed to belong to itself: the sandbars, the marshes, the mudflats, and the tidal channels with algae streaming in the ebb and flow were all formed and nourished by the river, subtle and evanescent as it was. The river made the horizon, since there was nothing to grow or build on that it couldn't take away on a windy April night. Against this simple background, the human body was plainly, rather painfully, visible again: a stick figure squinting in the glare, hopping across the mud, loitering at the edges of the sumac thickets that made the whole expanse seem a little like an image from *Heart of Darkness*. A thunderstorm came up, so we beached the boat and ran into the bushes. I hadn't seen before then that bolts of lightning reach to the ground, or that they are thick, like vines, and a brilliant rose-violet in color.

# Across the Okefenokee

Once in a while, a trip to the wilderness is like a vacation in some posh resort. You don't get caught in storms, devoured by insects, lost, sunburned, sick, frozen, or exhausted. Instead, everything seems designed to please you. Camp food tastes wonderful, travel is exhilarating instead of tiring, and the wilderness itself is entirely welcoming—strange and awesome, perhaps, but never ominous or depressing. Any wilderness trip that isn't a total disaster will include such pleasures, of course, but it's a rare one that doesn't include some moments of longing for the comforts and safety of civilization. Still, there are times when the wilderness seems to roll out a red carpet, to pamper visitors as though they were the most effete of Riviera sunbathers.

The last place I'd have expected to enjoy such deluxe accommodations was the Okefenokee Swamp in Georgia. Pogo aside, my early notions of the swamp were formed by a movie called *Black Fury,* which I saw at a Saturday matinee when I was seven. Actually, I didn't see the movie, just the preview, but that was enough. The hero was a burly, bearded character, but the swamp made short work of him. During the two or three minutes of the preview (and between wrestling bouts with an alligator and a black bear), it reduced him to a pale, sweating wreck, staggering in terror through endless corridors of cypress trunks and muck. Though it was enjoyable to watch all this on a movie screen, it didn't exactly prompt me to explore the swamp. Or perhaps it did. When I discovered that the U.S. Fish and Wildlife Service had developed a system of canoe trails across the Okefenokee, I sensed that I would someday have to give in to the lure of the swamp.

Giving in to the lure of the swamp wasn't so easy, though. I could have made reservations in most resorts with less trouble (albeit with more expense). The Okefenokee is a very popular place. I wrote in July to make reservations for October, but the swamp was all booked up. The Fish and Wildlife Service sensibly lets only one party stay at a campsite on a given night, so I had to settle for November. Then, two weeks before our trip was to begin, I was informed that there wasn't enough water in the swamp for the loop trip we'd planned, that we'd have to take another route. Arranging this involved several expensive telephone calls, but I finally got a permit to canoe from Kingfisher Landing on the east side of the swamp to Stephen Foster Recreation Area on the west side, a three-day trip.

It was a warm, sunny morning when we drove through the sandy pine woods toward the swamp. I had thought the woods would get deeper and gloomier as we approached, but it wasn't like that at all. Approaching the Okefenokee was a little like approaching the ocean. The sky seemed to expand around us, and there was a kind of sparkle to the air. At the water's edge, we looked down a canal through low, shrubby thickets and across an expanse of green grass and water that was broken only occasionally by islands of pines or bald cypress. Most of the east side of the Okefenokee is made up of such "prairies"—open stretches of grass and sedge that look like dry land until you step onto them and the waterlogged peat substrate begins to sink and quake. The name "Okefenokee" is from an Indian term meaning "place of trembling earth."

It was an alluring vista, into which we lost no time launching the canoe. I don't think I've experienced *less* gloomy surroundings than the Okefenokee prairies on that clear November day. They were covered with yellow flowers called tickseeds, apparently just an echo of the flowers that bloomed there in spring. Everything in the prairies was movement, light, clarity—rushes bending in the breeze, sunlight reflected from a million grass stems, water rippling under the canoe. The swamp water was brown-tinged, but there was nothing stagnant about it. The entire swamp flows like a river that has been spread out over a hundred thousand acres of white sand and peat, and if you are moving with the flow, you hardly have to paddle your canoe, just simply steer as the water carries you toward one of the rivers that drain the swamp.

Prairie colors were soft and bright—light green of grass and lily pads, blue-gray of Spanish moss, pink and pale blue of broomsedge. Dozens of red-veined pitcher plants thrust from the grass as though they were trumpets proclaiming the attractions of the place instead of traps for unwary insects. Even the smells were beautiful—sandy, resinous, peaty perfumes, constantly stirred to freshness by the breeze.

This description may seem exaggerated, but it isn't really. It *is* selective. There were a few hints of the punishment the swamp could administer to the unlucky. The wind rose and clouds gathered during the afternoon. I experienced a sinking sensation as I recalled that November is still pretty close to hurricane season. After lunch we passed through a stretch of peat "blowups" where swamp gas had forced a layer of peat to the surface of the canoe trail. It was like canoeing through soggy bran flakes, and I had visions of having to get out and drag the boat through the mire like Humphrey Bogart in *The African Queen*. But the blowups only lasted a few yards, and the sky cleared by late afternoon.

The swamp became even more beautiful as the sun declined and the wind died down. The water became absolutely smooth—a smoothness no lake or sea could ever match, unprotected as they are by the Okefenokee's screen of grasses and trees. It was dreamlike to glide over this smoothness, through a landscape that appeared to be woods and meadows but was actually a vast, hidden mirror of water flowing so silently and inconspicuously that one tended to forget its enormous volume and tensile strength.

As the sky began to turn red, we ran into a stretch of bay thickets, different from the prairies. The water in them seemed more "swampy," with clots of roots and mud protruding from it. Big schools of whirligig beetles revolved madly in dark coves, some so numerous that they made a sound like fat frying. The thickets were difficult to canoe through; there was much twisting and turning, scraping against branches and bumping into the bank. It began to get late, and we paddled hard enough to get a few nascent blisters but reached Maul Hammock, our first night's stopping place, in time to make camp.

We hadn't seen any alligators all day, which was disappointing—I'd had preconceptions of giant alligators disporting everywhere. As we glided into Maul Hammock Lake, though, a five-foot alligator made an alarmed squeaking sound and ran into the water, sinking out of sight in the usual manner of alligators: that is, very discreetly if not furtively. Its tail and body sank first, leaving only the two bumps of eyes and snout; then the eyes quietly disappeared and finally the snout, leaving only a few tiny bubbles to indicate there was large reptile close under the surface. This was the universal response of Okefenokee alligators to our approach, with two exceptions. A small alligator in the middle of the swamp seemed to feel that it could avoid us simply by submerging its head, lying in the water with tail and body fully exposed even when we drifted to within a few feet of it. A very large, algae-encrusted individual on the west side of the swamp clearly had no intention of submerging to avoid us, merely cruising out into deeper water when we passed, as though cannily seeking a position of advantage.

To return to Maul Hammock, the night we spent there was perhaps the liveliest I've experienced in a wilderness area. As we arrived, flocks of wood storks and white ibis were making croaking and grunting bedtime noises from a cypress grove across the lake, and sandhill cranes were bugling and honking in nearby Sapling Prairie. We'd seen several groups of cranes that afternoon, the first time I'd ever seen them, and it had been very exciting. Cranes are a kind of wilderness totem: you don't see them around civilized places as you do herons and egrets. They seem to live in another time—heavy, primitive birds, but with great dignity. The cranes we saw in the Okefenokee never hesitated at our approach as did other wading birds. They immediately flung themselves into the air, complaining loudly at our intrusion, and flew out of sight by the shortest possible route. We barely got close enough to see the red skin on their heads.

After the ibis, storks, and cranes had quieted down, crickets and grasshoppers still made a considerable din from the jungle-like vegetation of the hammock, and frogs began peculiar clacking choruses on the lake as the light faded. The frog choruses began abruptly, like a burst of applause, stopped just as abruptly a few minutes later, then started again on another part of the lily pad–covered lake. When it was quite dark, the *real* noise began—barred owls. I had heard barred owls before, but never from every patch of trees within earshot. At least three owls were calling around the lake, and many more in the distance. Carried across the vast watery surface of the swamp, the calls sounded uncannily loud and clear. The typical hoots of barred owls are usually transcribed as "who cooks for you? who cooks for *you* all?" but these culinary inquiries are varied with an incredible range of hilariously macabre sounds—wails, howls, yelps, and cackles.

This din went on at intervals through the night, and was complemented by splashes, gurgles, and liquid murmuring sounds from the lake. When I shone a flashlight out over the water, the blackness was dotted with round red reflections—alligator eyes. Just after our evening meal, when I first shone the light, there was one set of alligator eyes on the lake (you actually see two reflections for each eye—the bright red real eye and the pale yellow reflection of it in the water). When I shone the light again just before we crawled into our sleeping bags, there were at least half a dozen sets of eyes. The alligators paid no attention to us, though. The only disturbers of our sleep were a cotton rat the size of a squirrel that clanked our cooking gear, then galloped off as I shone the flashlight on it, and a few mosquitoes—last survivors of hordes that must have made the swamp a considerably less comfortable place a month or so previously.

The swamp seemed a completely different place when we woke up at Maul Hammock on the second day of our trip. The bright clear air that had made the wet prairies and cypress groves seem more like some pristine alpine wilderness than a southern lowland swamp was replaced by a thick gray mist. Heavy dew dripped from the roof of the wooden shelter we were camped on, and the air was muffled by the fog. Swamp water that had been blue and sparkling the day before was now black and opaque, and the cypress grove across the lake that had glowed rosily in the sunset now loomed spectrally. It was a little like one of those old stories of enchantment in which the hero goes to sleep in a garden of delights and wakes up under a gallows. White ibis flying across the lake from their roost in the cypress looked and sounded like carrion crows.

The fog dissipated with surprising swiftness, though, and by the time we had set off westward across Sapling Prairie, the swamp had regained the breezy, sparkling aspect of the day before. The ibis that had croaked so mournfully in the fog now ran about cheerfully in the mud, probing with their long, decurved bills for small crustaceans or insect larvae. The white-plumaged, red-billed mature ibis fluttered away like giant butterflies as we approached, but the brown-plumaged juveniles just stood and watched us with curiosity. When we reached the other side of Sapling Prairie, the swamp changed again—a more permanent change this time. The water began to flow west toward the Suwanee River instead of east toward the St. Mary's River. We had reached the "summit" of the swamp, the low ridge that separates a watershed draining into the Gulf of Mexico from one emptying into the Atlantic. The expansive, sunlit prairies began to dwindle into spreading groves of cypress, antechambers to the dense stands of mature cypress and swamp hardwoods that cover much of the western Okefenokee.

There was still no sense of gloom or oppression on entering the cypress groves. There was a subtle, flowery smell and an arboretum-like variety of interesting plants—palmetto, white and yellow water lilies, pickerelweeds, pondweeds, and a rush-like submerged plant that grew so thickly on the bottom of the trail that canoeing over it was something like trying to paddle through a vat of spaghetti.

But there was an element of grotesquerie in the cypress swamp. The water contained roots that looked like severed limbs or alligator backs (the similarity between swamp roots and alligators somehow seemed more than accidental), and lichen-covered snags and cypress knees sometimes resembled hoary phantoms rising from the ooze. The trees themselves had a grotesque side as well as a graceful, colorful one. There seemed to be no such thing as a "young" cypress, only big ones and small ones. The small cypresses were as gnarled, gray-barked, and lichen- and spanish moss-covered as their presumed parents.

The water was deeper in the cypress stands, and we encountered more small aquatic creatures than we had in the prairies. There were tiny brown frogs so small that they could hop around on the water surface like bugs. Much larger speckle-bellied frogs were extremely shy and wary, which seemed sensible behavior considering the sizeable population of wading birds, red-shouldered hawks, barred owls, and other frog-eating predators in the swamp. Perhaps fleeing from some underwater predator, a small pickerel jumped right into the canoe with us. We threw it back after some idle thoughts about eating it ourselves—it was probably under the legal limit anyway. One or two of the tiny brown frogs also jumped into the canoe, then jumped out again with surprisingly high leaps.

The vegetation became denser during the afternoon, and the trail became narrower and more weedy. Sometimes we had to crouch and pull the canoe through the shrubbery with our hands, and the trail seemed about to peter out as though we'd taken a wrong turn. I didn't like the idea of having to paddle back against the current and flowing weeds. We had visions of cottonmouth moccasins hanging from the thickets we were struggling through, but we didn't encounter any; didn't see *any* snakes in the swamp, in fact. At one place a fallen log blocked the trail, but we managed to maneuver around it without even getting our feet wet.

In the late afternoon, the trail opened out again, and we started passing stretches of cypress and big hardwoods that looked almost like dry land. An anhinga (a relative of the cormorant that is also called a snakebird because of its long sinuous neck) and a wood stork flew away through the trees, but birdlife wasn't as conspicuous in the cypress as in the prairies. There were chickadees and titmice in the trees, and an occasional robin call added an incongruously suburban note to the primeval setting, but the flocks of wading birds seemed to avoid the big trees. One possible reason for this avoidance appeared as we passed into Big Water Lake (more a bayou than a lake, actually, a stately aisle of dark water lined with giant cypress, sweetgum, and maple) and began to see alligators about every fifty yards, each one performing its discrete disappearing act for our benefit. It seemed ludicrous to us for such powerful creatures to be so furtive, but it might have seemed more sinister to a heron or ibis. A barred owl, perched in a tree beside the water, watched us in the disconcerting way owls have of turning their heads at seemingly impossible angles to their bodies. It let us drift quite close, then dropped down into a small waterway beneath the tree, perhaps to take a drink or catch a frog.

We spent our second night in the swamp beside a little canal off Big Water. The camp was surrounded by a dense stand of small cypress. It wasn't as picturesque as the previous night's, or as noisy, although we heard cranes bugling from nearby Floyd's Prairie, and of course barred owls. It was a warm night, so invertebrates were active. A steady stream of moths knocked their heads against our Coleman lantern, including some big white ones with handsome black markings. At one point I thought it had started to rain, but the "raindrops" proved to be dozens of tiny mayflies rising and falling on their diaphanous wings in the lamplight. Late in the evening, a large black, yellow, and orange spider crept into the circle of light, which seemed to confuse it, since it made no attempt to capture any of the moths or craneflies that clustered on the boards. Despite the abundance of other insects, mosquitoes were still pleasantly scarce.

The next morning was misty again, a light mist through which a crescent moon was visible just above the reddish-brown needles of the cypresses (bald-cypress is one of the few deciduous conifers—the Okefenokee trees had changed color at this time of year, but hadn't yet lost their needles). As the mist cleared, we became aware that a red-shouldered hawk was perched across the canal from us, a disheveled individual that gazed morosely into the water and paid us no heed as we loaded the canoe. As we pushed off to leave, a mockingbird appeared and flew to a branch beside the hawk, eyeing the much larger bird intently and aggressively. It was so obviously eager to fight for possession of the area that the hawk flew meekly away.

We drifted back onto Big Water, which became narrower and blended into the forest so that we were canoeing around the cypress trunks and knees. (Cypress knees are knobby growths that protrude above the water from the tree's roots. Their function is unclear—possibly to absorb oxygen.) We glided past a white-tailed doe before either we or the deer were aware of one another's presence. Seeing us, she bounded and splashed along the water's edge for a few yards, then stopped and eyed us, not much afraid. As the day warmed, alligators appeared to share sunning logs with black and yellow turtles ranging from matchbox to washtub size.

We had seen beer cans floating in Big Water the day before, evidence that motorboats used it. Now we encountered the first human we saw in the swamp, a gap-toothed, spindly fisherman who looked as though he might have grown up in the vicinity. He was friendly; said the fish weren't biting. I wondered if he might have been a former alligator poacher, a common activity in the swamp before classification of the alligator as an endangered species ended the alligator leather industry. The rebound of the alligator population after the poaching ended seems to have awed the slightly intimidated wildlife managers, but we didn't think there were too many alligators in the swamp.

We met two of the wildlife refuge personnel (the Okefenokee is a U.S. Wildlife Refuge and also a federal wilderness area under provisions of the Wilderness Act of 1964) a little farther west. They were on their way to check the trail east of Big Water, some Boy Scouts having complained of obstructions. They answered my questions about the contrast between the open prairies on the east side of the swamp and the cypress forest on the west genially if somewhat inconclusively. It seems there are two possible explanations. Either the east side is geologically younger than the west, having been seashore and salt marsh while the west side was already freshwater swamp—or fires in the east side have burned off most of the woody vegetation as well as several feet of underlying peat, making the area too soggy to support forest, at least for the present. The older of the two refuge people told us that crossing the prairies in a pole boat had been easy in the 1930s, but that they are noticeably drier today.

The day grew hot, and we began to feel just the faintest touch of overexposure to the sun when we entered a wide, apparently artificial waterway for the last mile of our trip. The Okefenokee is scarred in several places with abandoned canals—monuments to the nineteenth-century drainage projects, one of which ended, as the story goes, when an elderly ex-slave pointed out to the engineers that the water in their canal was flowing *into* the swamp, not out of it. When we paddled into Stephen Foster Recreation Area and stepped onto truly dry earth for the first time in three days, I probed my psyche for feelings of disappointment that we had not had to surmount any hardships or dangers in getting across the swamp. But there were no such feelings. The Okefenokee is such a beautiful place that you don't get bored, no matter how gently it treats you.

# Japan's Wild Nature

This clear bright pond
Ruffled in the wind;
Pines that nod from their crags in greeting;
Rocks shining from the river bottom beneath drifting
    watery mirrors;
Scattered clouds that cloak the summits in shadows;
The half-risen moon which lights the vales,
When from tree to tree dart crying birds:
To these will I abandon, will I entrust my life.
—Isonolcami no Yalcatsugu (729–81)

Translated by Burton Watson

JAPAN has perhaps come closer than any other nation to making nature the center of its aesthetic. There's something exceptional about a culture that has arts of moon and firefly watching and insect listening as well as landscape painting and poetry. I had mixed feelings about this when I had an opportunity to go to Japan for a couple of weeks. On the one hand, I looked forward to seeing the landscapes of the paintings and poems. On the other, I was afraid the Japanese had made such an art out of their land that it would contain nothing I could relate to directly—that the whole place would be a kind of giant landscape scroll, woodblock album, or Zen garden. Much as I like landscape scrolls, woodblock albums, and Zen gardens, a whole country of them somehow doesn't appeal. Art is a nice place to visit, but I wouldn't want to live there.

There was nothing in the least "Japanese" about the landscape over which our Thai Airlines jet flew on its way to Tokyo, though. It was a tangle of steep, forested ridges that might have been in North Carolina. The only odd note was that some of the ridges had golf courses on their tops, which is not what one would find on a North Carolina ridgetop. But only a fifth of Japan is flat, and almost all of that is used for buildings or growing food, so golf courses—which are very popular in Japan—have to go somewhere. The forests that shared the ridgetops with the golf courses didn't look particularly natural— even-aged stands of cedar evidently planted for reforestation—but they didn't look like landscape scrolls. Japan was a real place. Tokyo certainly didn't look very "Japanese." Except for its newness, tidiness, and "icanji"-lettered billboards, it might have been Baltimore, especially seen through its midsummer petrochemical haze. Fragments of the natural world in Tokyo were about the same as one would find in any modern city. Robust, heavy-beaked crows sat on telephone poles, oblivious to the rapids of Datsuns and Toyotas that roared beneath them. Brown jays and wood pigeons squawked and cooed respectively in parks (but there was a complete absence of squirrels in city parks or elsewhere, so far as I could see during my short visit). Sidewalks were frequented by the usual sparrows, starlings (brown and tan instead of black like ours), and blue city pigeons. I suppose there must be a point at which human congestion crowds out even sparrows and starlings, but that point hasn't been reached yet even in Tokyo.

Japan and nature reasserted themselves when we went to a little town called Yumigahama on the Izu Penninsula, seventy miles from Tokyo. The roads on the way were so narrow and winding that mirrors had been set up at every curve to let drivers know if another car was coming. It seemed likely that the Japanese mountains have kept Tokyo at bay to some extent. Neither the nature nor the Japan at Yumigahama were quite what I'd expected, though.

I'd always thought of Japan as a cool-temperate place, but Yumigahama was a lively, disheveled subtropical resort town that reminded me of Puerto Vallarta: little, winding streets piled with crates of fish, mocking children, thousands of scuttling, bright-red land crabs that blanched yellow and pinched fiercely if picked up. Brown hawks called kites joined the crows on telephone poles, the birds evidently performing the same garbage removal function of "zopilotes" in Mexican towns.

The crescent-shaped beach was the dirtiest I've ever seen, a dense mosaic of Styrofoam, tar, old campfires, cans, and bottles that came as a surprise after Tokyo's cleanliness. There'd been a typhoon the day before, which partly explained the mess, but all that crap had to come from somewhere. The Japanese seem to have an opposite approach to throwaway culture than we do. We litter city streets, but tend to keep beaches and other out-of-the-way places clean. I suppose the Japanese approach is more rational—one generally spends more time on city streets than on beaches—but it's still a little uncomfortable to set up your beach blanket, radio, suntan oil, and other accessories in the remains of last night's Japanese equivalent of a wienie roast.

Outside the high rise-dotted resort area, things were more as I'd expected. The small river valley that ran into the hills was still an exquisite network of stone-diked rice paddies full of crabs, red crayfish, and frogs, brooded over by dark herons. A shrine on a hillside hinted at a very ancient integration of land and culture. A recently restored wooden temple at the base of the hill gave way to a long flight of mossy steps heavily over-shadowed by huge cedars and hardwoods, which led up to a strange little cedar-board box of a building, decayed and rat-holed, but somehow full of presence. A tiny brown frog hopped across the moss like a character from a folktale. Off to one side was a wild, marshy meadow, evidently left to itself for religious reasons, and probably representing an economic sacrifice in flatland-poor Japan. It seemed a very quiet, secret place; and although it was neglected compared with the temples and gardens of Nara or Kyoto, it struck me as a truer harmony of wildness and artifice. It was only a few yards from a tile-roofed hamlet full of television aerials and Honda bikes, but the two didn't really seem at odds.

The hills and ocean headlands above Yumigahama were buzzing with life, literally. Slender green cicadas made the biggest racket I've ever heard from insects, a deafening whir that swept over the slopes in waves, so that we would be standing in perfect silence at one moment, then be engulfed by a rush of noise that left our ears ringing (Yukio Mishima gives cicadas a lot of space in one of his novels, *Spring Snow*, I believe.) The Izu hills also supported the showiest butterflies I've seen. I spent most of an afternoon on a rocky knoll, watching them flutter over the dwarf woodland of chestnut, live oak, ailanthus, rhododendron, and wild hydrangea that covered the headlands. There were huge black and white swallowtails with a bright red blush on their lower wings, and a jet black species with spots of iridescent turquoise. In the weeds beside the path, a pair of red, green, yellow, and black mottled snakes was copulating. Their brilliant red was the same as that of the crabs and crayfish—I think it's called Chinese red, the same color one sees on lacquered objects. I wondered if some element in the soil caused so many creatures to be that color.

The Izu coastline was pure Japanese blockprint—little islands with fantastic rocks and silhouetted pines; a pale, greenish-blue sea; distant ships; graceful lines of seabirds and dolphins (as yet unliquidated by fisheries authorities). But the quaintness was complicated when we followed the beach around a rocky point and came to a cove that must have been a World War II military installation—huge concrete abutments rising from the water, now covered with chitons, anemones, and other tidepool creatures, but obviously not built to enhance the scenery. The cove reminded me of one of those paintings one sees from the People's Republic of China that depicts mountain scenes in perfect Sung Dynasty style but also happens to contain hydroelectric dams and ranks of high-tension cables. Imagine a Hokusai print with a submarine installation in it and you have that cove.

Monkeys live on the Izu Peninsula, and we stopped at a Japanese national park service designated "monkey habitat" on the way back to Tokyo. It wasn't where I'd have expected to see monkeys. In fact, it was a lot like Golden Gate National Recreation Area, with brushy cliffs dropping steeply to the ocean. The monkeys lived on the cliffs, although it wasn't exactly a wilderness life. They drank from the water faucets provided for visitors, hung around the food concession and eagerly tried to intimidate us tourists into handing over edibles, the presence of which they could discern from a person's bearing, and which they would go after whether in hands, purses, or pockets. They made the Yosemite black bears seem downright reclusive. I got the feeling they would just as soon have gotten in the car with us and gone to Tokyo to take on the restaurants and markets.

A couple of hundred miles inland from Tokyo is Shiga Heights, a segment of the massif that cuts across most of central Honshu. We spent two nights there at an enormous high-rise ski and hot springs resort built on top of a gorge. The parking lot was the only flat place for miles. It was as subalpine as the Izu Peninsula had been subtropical, and the slopes around the resort were covered with lush hemlock, fir, beech, and birch forest. The wildflowers reminded me of California backpacking—fireweed, bunchberry, tiger lily, gentian. We saw large black and white birds quite similar to the Clark's crows of the High Sierra, and the woods were full of little chickadee- and nuthatch-like songbirds. The only distinctly oriental note I could see was a thick underbrush of bamboo that grew almost everywhere.

Shiga Heights is part of Josin-Etsu Highlands National Park, but the Japanese have a somewhat different concept of the national park than we Americans. There was a dammed reservoir and evidence of large-scale mining within an hour's walk of the resort, which itself wasn't what Americans would expect in a park unless they start building high rises in Yosemite. I can't read Japanese, but there didn't seem to be any clear park boundaries—no ubiquitous wooden signs or Smokey-hatted rangers. Hiking trails were not maintained although they were so heavily used they'd been beaten into avenues of mud and puddles. Switchbacks apparently were unheard of. The trail downhill from a ridgetop we'd climbed was a dizzying mudslide whereon the presence of other hikers were belied by their thumps, grunts, and curses as they slipped and slid on the slick clay. A peak visible from the ridgetop had an unbroken line of colorfully clad climbers—probably a tour group—from its base to its summit.

There did seem to be some wilderness at Shiga Heights, though we didn't have time to get into it. Beyond the ridge we hiked was a steep, faraway gorge with no sign of human occupancy, just unbroken forest and dragons of mist crawling up the ravines. Wild boars and small bears supposedly live in the area, though we saw no signs of them. We did catch a glimpse of a pine marten, a creature I'd be excited to see in any wildland. Maybe there are plans to build a resort in that gorge too, but for the present it seems that even a country as densely settled—both physically and culturally—as Japan has yet to exhaust completely its wild nature. Which means, among other things, that the nature-centered tradition of Japanese art still has some room to grow.

# The Big Two-Hearted
Wilderness

THE Beartooth-Absaroka Wilderness Area in Montana north
of Yellowstone Park contains two very different mountain
ranges. The Beartooth Range is a massif of granite peaks so
rugged as to be nearly impenetrable. No trails lead across its
spine, and some of it is still virtually unexplored. The Absaroka, on the other hand, is composed mostly of soft, red volcanic stone, so it is gentler than the Beartooth. Its summits are
rounded humps or buttes instead of crags, and look more invit-
ing than forbidding—the backpacker feels an urge to climb up
and roll around on them. Broad river valleys and pine-forested
ridges surround the summits. Absaroka rivers meander sunnily
through wide meadows and willow flats; Beartooth rivers rush
darkly through deep, spruce-hung gorges.

My wife, Betsy Kendall, and I backpacked for a week in each
of the ranges this summer, and we felt we were in two very
different countries although the trail into the Absaroka came
within a dozen map miles of the one into the Beartooth. The
Absaroka had a spacious, Old West quality about it—there was
usually a herd of horses (saddle stock from local dude ranches)
grazing a meadow beneath the eroded buttes. In the glow of
evening, the Absaroka landscape had all the arcadian elements
of nineteenth-century Romantic painting—a few picturesque
conifers framing the foreground, horses running across the mid-

dle distance, a plume of blue smoke from a campfire, the gigantic but softly lit summits in the background.

The Beartooth might have been in Transylvania—there was something chilly and eerie about the range. The crags crowded in too closely for the right kind of Romantic effect, as though the painter's skills were a bit on the primitive side, as though he didn't know just how to mix his colors right to give the desired edenic impression. The dark fir and spruce forest often seemed quite empty of life. We'd spend an evening watching the sunlight recede up the granite walls, and there would be no sound except the wind, no movement except perhaps a nighthawk circling high above the Stillwater River.

We came to a few places in the Beartooth where the Stillwater gorge opened into meadows and marshes with a fair amount of wildlife—beaver, a solitary moose cow, white-tailed and mule deer, red squirrels, pikas on the talus slopes (short-eared, alpine rabbit relatives), a marten hunting pikas and squirrels, to the vociferous complaints of both prey species. One night a roly-poly flying squirrel visited our camp and helped itself to a lemon crunch granola bar from our food stuffsack, chewing an excessively large hole in the sack in the process. It was quite bold, hanging upside down from a branch to eye us when we turned a flashlight on it, and whispering to itself. But our general impression of life in the Beartooth was "diminuendo." It was rough country, and probably didn't offer much food.

In the Absaroka there was so much wildlife that it was a little intimidating. It seemed we couldn't go for a walk outside our camp in the evening without bumping into a moose or two—or three—enormous, full-antlered bull moose that tiptoed away into the forest so quietly that it seemed they must be up to something. They weren't much inclined to flee from us, and we never knew when a moose would suddenly appear.

One mosquito-ridden evening (the mosquito was a life form both ranges had in abundance), we sat on a cliff and watched an elk herd wander across a distant meadow, the calves gamboling around the cows, the antlered bulls keeping a little apart. The silhouetted herd might have walked off the walls of the Lascaux caverns, and seemed to inhabit a different planet from elk we saw later in Yellowstone Park, which were being pursued across the meadows by camera-wielding park visitors. (It was almost impossible to focus on wildlife in the park because the behavior of the humans was so arresting and ubiquitous.)

We felt jostled on all sides by wildlife in the Absaroka. We saw hardly any sign of the vaunted grizzly—and only one small black bear that I startled away from a collision course with our tent one evening—but thoughts of huge, snarling grizzly heads tended to drift through our minds as we crawled into our sleeping bags. (Getting into a sleeping bag evokes peculiarly mingled feelings of security and helplessness.) Quiet afternoons were sometimes interrupted by raucous squawks that might have been made by gangs of teenage delinquents. In a sense they were. Ravens had just fledged their broods, and the fledglings were following their elders around noisily demanding to be fed as though they were still nestlings. Even the Absaroka trees made their presence felt intimidatingly. Many were dead or dying from the harsh winters, and they kept falling down with startling crashes and cracks.

The climax to all this liveliness came when we spent two days beside a lake that turned out to be occupied by a family of otters (along with the customary moose, in this case a bull that made a point of urinating conspicuously into a little stream that fed the lake). I was sitting at our campsite after breakfast when a sleek brown head appeared from the water perhaps ten feet away and looked me over. I was judged harmless, evidently, since the otter promptly went about its affairs as though I wasn't there. It crawled out on a raft of driftwood for a moment, then slipped back underwater. A few minutes later, it reappeared in a patch of rushes across an inlet. Another adult otter joined it, and the pair touched noses and groomed one another for a little while, then swam away to the other side of the lake.

In late morning the otters reappeared with their two offspring. They swam around the lake toward our camp like a miniature pod of dolphins, alternately diving and surfacing in the same way as dolphins swim, the baby otters keeping up with their parents quite well although they were only a third as large. The family left the water at the rush patch across the inlet, where one of the adults apparently caught a snake or frog and quickly ate it as the youngsters squirmed and pushed at their parent much as human toddlers do. They clearly wanted attention more than a piece of frog.

The family left the rushes and swam across the inlet toward us, climbing out on a fallen log that extended from our campsite into the water. The hungry adult fished a very dead trout from a patch of rush and ate it, while one of the youngsters continued to pester him (or her). The other youngster investigated a floating clot of algae, and the other parent stayed in the water, surreptitiously peering at us with perhaps a trace of anxiety. These pursuits occupied the otters for about five minutes, then the parents and attention-hungry baby swam out of sight around a point, leaving the algae student behind. It realized that it was alone a moment later and hurried off after the others. That was the last we saw of them.

By Walt Disney standards, these otters didn't quite measure up. They didn't put on the clown show we've come to expect from "true life adventures." The impression I got was of creatures of very respectable strength and vitality going about their lives in a businesslike way. I felt I could have some insight into their curiosity and their evident pleasure in being alive in a suitable place for otters, but there was an otherness about them that reflected the more obvious nonhumanity of weather-beaten trees, secretive moose, and raucous ravens. They were very much their own beings, and this was a little hard to swallow. It asked more for the respect that one owes to an unfamiliar person than the love one gives to a pet or a friend.

This encounter shed a new light on something that has bothered me for many years. During the height of the "ecology movement," some friends who had just bought land in the country acquired a baby otter. I don't know where it came from, but it was about the age of the young otters at the Absaroka lake. It had probably been weaned too early for its emotional health. Having read *Ring of Bright Water,* (Gavin Maxwell's memoir on raising pet otters), we were all prepared for a thoroughly delightful creature, a super pet. But the baby otter wasn't having any of that. It had its own otter needs, and was not concerned with charming us.

The baby otter wanted attention *all* the time, and its outcries on being denied it were unceasingly and surprisingly loud and shrill. It wanted continual body contact, and it liked to crawl under clothes—but it also expressed frequent displeasure by biting. It bit me when I tried to take a cooked chicken bone away from it, and I can testify that even a baby otter bite is something to fear. It bit everybody—dogs, cats, children, adults—and people became afraid to touch it, which only made it even unhappier. By human standards the baby otter was impossible—a brat—and after a few weeks my friends returned it to its original "owners," to everyone's remorseful relief.

Watching the otter family in the Absaroka, I realized why we had failed with the small captive. Humans don't really have enough focus on otter needs to raise a baby otter properly. Of course, otters have been raised by humans, but I suspect that the products of such upbringings are lacking in certain otter qualities, just as the humans that were raised by wolves lacked the human faculty of speech, lacked in some cases even the potentiality for developing that faculty once they'd been returned to society.

The idea that we can tame any animal at will is based on a rather arrogant assumption of superiority—an assumption that human intelligence transcends any special qualities or needs that another species might have. Historians make much of "man's domestication of the animals," but domestic animals are separated from wild animals by as great a gulf as we are separated from the Cro-Magnons. It's likely that there was as much symbiotic coevolution in the domestication process as purposeful taming. Humans and animals that became domesticated had certain needs in common, and shared certain benefits. Dogs found hunting partners in humans, and when cows and sheep settled down to live with their hominid predators, they at least found protection from their leonine and hyenid ones.

The vast majority of animals simply have no business living with humans. The conclusion that Barry Lopez (*Wolves and*

*Men*) drew from keeping wolves as pets was that he had gained a great deal from the association, but the wolves had gained nothing. The notion of universal friendship between humans and animals is not as old as that of universal friendship among humans, but I suspect they're equally treacherous. Both imply a fatal tendency to righteous anger when friendship is not accepted with grateful alacrity. With animals as with humans, friendship is not as important in the long run as the respecting of boundaries, the acceptance of limits. For me this is the most important reason for having wilderness areas—they provide the boundaries that make respect possible.

# This Tangled Brilliance

Summer sunsets last much of the night on the fjords of southeastern Alaska. The sun does not stay up all night, as it does above the Arctic Circle, but darkness is very late in descending.

A little shoreline meadow on Stephens Passage glowed in the slanting sunlight of a late afternoon in July. The wet climate and long days had packed the slope between the salt water of the passage and the trees of Tongass National Forest with oversized cow parsnips, dandelions, and ferns. Pale paintbrush, a wildflower whose greenish-yellow bracts are barely tinged with the scarlet of its mountain relatives, grew several feet tall. The dark purple blossoms of Indian rice (so called for the masses of small, edible tubers at its roots) stood out like dark stars against this tangled brilliance.

The shade of the forest's Sitka spruce, western hemlock, and alder seemed very dark in contrast to the meadow, but there were flowers there too—orderly beds of white clintonia and spiky devil's club. A small porcupine was climbing one of the alders. When it reached a height to its liking, it pulled a leafy branch to its mouth with its forepaws. The hairs on its forehead drooped and nodded as it munched the leaves. Its footprints in the soft earth at the base of the tree resembled a human baby's.

The meadow was rich in odors as the afternoon breezes stirred the air. The forest exhaled dim odors of mold and spruce gum that mingled with spicy meadow herb fragrances and fishy, rocky smells from the shore. The tide was out, and the sea smells were accentuated by piles of damp seaweed and the decomposing remains of a harbor seal.

The meadow overlooked a small cove, a crescent of sand and granite boulders overgrown with rockweed and red algae. Both ends of the crescent were walled with steeply upended rock strata from which the tides had eroded the boulders. Little tidepools lay in the crevices—reminders that the sea had released the rocks only temporarily. Shore crabs with neat, white leg-joints sidled about in the pools, and tiny yellow blennies—fish especially adapted to life in tidepools—hid in the rockweed. They were slender as eels and so well camouflaged that only their movements revealed them.

Another species of blenny that lived in the tidepools had evolved a very different camouflage strategy. They resembled the members of a large mussel colony, being exactly the right dark blue color when they lay in the shadows of the colony (although they were light green in sunlight), and having on their bodies blotches of bone white that perfectly mimicked the barnacles growing on the mussels. They are aggressive fish, chasing their companions about their small niche and rising to the surface at every falling speck. Soon they would have to retire deeper into the mussel beds, however; the tide was beginning to come in, bringing larger predators.

The tide came in gently because the cove was screened from the open Pacific by the massive bulk of Admiralty Island, visible a few miles across Stephens Passage. As the tide slowly rose in the cove, the snow cornices on Admiralty's distant peaks became tinged with orange. The island became a backdrop for a crowded stage as dozens of shoreline creatures came out for the evening feeding period.

A flock of gulls circled above a school of fish, and a bald eagle flew past them toward its nest in a spruce just north of the cove. The eagle whistled and chattered like an overgrown songbird as it wheeled about the untidy platform of sticks built halfway up the tree. Just off the cove a guillemot in black and white summer plumage stretched its wings, then dove underwater. Two gray-headed arctic loons sat placidly on the surface.

A humpback whale spouted in the deep water. The sound of its exhalation reached the cove several seconds after the white spume and dark back had subsided into the quiet water. The little guillemot surfaced. Gull cries drifted across the water. On the shore, a strangely bedraggled red squirrel ran along one of the big drift logs that separated the meadow from the beach. It passed this way most evenings. When it reached the end of the log, it followed a well-beaten trail back into the trees.

The light on the meadow and its surrounding trees grew intense as the sun sank toward the Admiralty peaks. A blue-needled spruce sapling seemed to crackle with electricity at the top of the meadow. The granite boulders on the shore took on an orange glow, and the snowfields on Admiralty began to turn pink. A raven croaked in the trees.

Three whales surfaced in quick succession. One of them held its flukes in the air for a long moment before sliding ponderously out of sight. The gull flock had drifted westward, and two eagles appeared to prowl along its edges. One of the eagles swooped and stole a fish from a gull, then fled in the direction of the nest north of the cove. Three gulls pursued a little way, screeching in annoyance, then gave up and flew eastward over the meadow. There was a rocky inlet in that direction where tired gulls could rest.

The gentle rise of the tide had been accelerating, and all at once the rockweed that had been drying in the sun was waving underwater. At the same time, the sun began to leave the cove. The light weakened and faded first on the sand and granite, then on the meadow. It lingered on the trees, though, and clouds of excited midges danced in its brilliance. The air grew cooler, and a breeze arose to ruffle the newly risen water. It carried a salty smell deep into the trees.

There was an abrupt fading of the light. Shadows crept to the treetops in a few minutes. The sun had set on the cove, although it still shone full on the mountains of the Glass Peninsula of Admiralty Island. The circling gulls appeared black against the illuminated peaks. The bald eagle that remained was distinguishable from the gulls by its longer, slower-moving wings.

The breeze died down, and the water of Stephens Passage became very smooth, mirroring the orange of the sky and the silver of the peaks. Sounds were emphatic in the stillness. A squirrel scolded in the trees. A fish jumped, then jumped again. A boat passed along the shore, heading north to Juneau. After it was out of sight, its wake splashed into the cove, tossing tufts of salt rush that grew at the water's edge. Even the rustle of a vole running through the meadow seemed loud. It was getting chilly, and no insect calls masked the other sounds.

The bald eagle left the gull flock and headed for the nest. Larger size and harsher cries identified it as the female of the pair. The chatter of the circling gulls sounded clearly over a mile of water. Two ravens flew over the cove, calling softly to one another. Their calls were so precisely enunciated and inflected that they might have been conversing.

"Kah. Koo-ah pah."

"Kapa. Koo-ra ka."

The shadows reached timberline on the Admiralty peaks, intensifying the contrast of forest and snowfield. The sky was red at the horizon, and the water paled from silver to platinum. The darkening had slowed considerably, however, and the rosy light stayed on the mountaintops a long time. Small clouds appeared, also rose-colored, and drifted eastward above the peaks.

A whale reared its bulk halfway out of the passage, making an explosive sound as it toppled back into the quiet water.

"Whump!"

The harsh cry of the female eagle came from the nest. The male eagle was flying over the cove at that moment, and he turned his head to glance back at his mate before veering across the water toward the gulls. A pair of guillemots fluttered along the shore and landed in the cove. The dove-sized, penguinlike birds rested on the water for a moment, ducking their heads with quick, rhythmic movements as though to make sure their feathers were fully waterproofed. Then they dived underwater in search of fish.

Colors shifted again as the light faded from the highest peaks. The little clouds on the horizon darkened to purple, the mountains to blue, and the water reflected them to green. For a moment, a jet climbing from Juneau caught the sunlight, and it left an indigo vapor trail across the sky. Away from the green land shadows, the passage waters glowed a very faint orange.

The final descent of the sun affected the gulls. They stopped fishing and began to circle upward in a column that soon rose high above the peaks. The male eagle remained among them, which seemed a not-altogether intelligent thing to do since there were no more fish to steal. Gulls swooped at him from time to time, but he merely ducked away. Perhaps he simply enjoyed being part of the ascending throng.

Suddenly the entire southwestern sky turned bright coral except for the dark seam of the jet vapor trail. Two swallows flitted past the cove, and one of the guillemots rose from the water and flew after them. The white of the guillemots' wings was still discernible, but the trees around the cove and the outline of the distant mountains were becoming vague. The pink sky faded to dull violet as suddenly as it had flared up.

The breeze came up again, raising leaden swells along the shoreline of the cove. A mink emerged from the forest and loped down to the water's edge, making tiny scampering sounds on the sand, driftwood, and stones as it hurried along. It didn't pause to look about or even sniff the ground. Like the red squirrel, the mink had a habit of passing this way at a certain time of evening. It followed the same well-beaten trail back into the forest. It was a diminutive predator, and seemed hardly larger than the squirrel.

The alder trees tossed in the breeze, but the spruces and hemlocks only stirred stiffly and sighed. Grunts and crunching sounds from one alder indicated that the small porcupine was still feeding, oblivious of the gathering darkness. Darkness was welcome to the deer mice that lived in the forest; the meadow's edge resounded with patterings and bumps as they emerged to look for seeds and berries.

A buoy lit up across the passage. The water was dim and gray now, a gulf broken only occasionally by the fluke of a spouting whale. The whales' ponderous breathing sounded close in the dimness, as though the great animals were rising just outside the cove.

The tide was in. It covered the sand beach completely, and its wavelets lapped at the driftwood logs. The sloping garden of wildflowers was a vague, greenish mass beneath the black of the trees. Some buzzing creature, sphinx moth or hummingbird, paused above a lacy cow-parsnip umbel for a moment.

The seam of the vapor trail was reversed—a pale streak against the dark sky. Directly above the cove, the first small star began to shine. It was past midnight.

# III  NATURAL HISTORY
# AND CONSERVATION

# Ecological Imperialism

I CAN'T get over a certain uneasiness at being by-lined as "The Naturalist." It is one of the few titles in modern society that requires—and consequently bestows—no official sanction. One can get a college degree as a biologist or ecologist, but not as a naturalist. There's something of the eighteenth century about "naturalist" that cuts it off from the nine-to-five world of jobs and professions. People tend to associate it with a romantic, preindustrial concept of Nature. Sometimes I feel embarrassed to be living in the twentieth century at all, as when friends or acquaintances are surprised or disappointed at finding me doing something "unnatural" like reading a murder mystery or living in Oakland. Linnaeus and Rousseau didn't *really* invent nature, though, and if a naturalist lacks official sanction, he or she ought to have in compensation the freedom to approach nature as the universal array of phenomena that it is, not just as material for the nine-to-five world's vacation fantasies.

All of this is by way of rationalization for writing about one of my favorite unnatural phenomena—television. As Chance the gardener says in *Being There:* "I like to watch." It's not that I'm a fiend. My case is fairly normal, even abstemious. My father insisted he was "waiting for color" until I was ten, so I arrived fairly late at close symbiosis with *Ozzie and Harriet, Wonderful World of Disney, Father Knows Best,* and *Shock Theater,* and it was not too long before puberty drove me back into the real world. Since then, long periods of abstinence have alternated with mild addiction whenever there was a tube within reach. I can't live with a television set and not become mildly addicted, which is why I often haven't had one, and why I'm mildly addicted now that I do have one, having been lured into the purchase by perfidious Albion in the guise of *Monty Python* and *Masterpiece Theater.*

All of this may not seem particularly appropriate to a nature piece, but I'm coming to that. First, I want to say that I can't stand most of the nature programs on television. I'd much rather watch Lou Grant than undergo Marlon Perkins's maunderings as he lassoes giraffes or Jean Jacques Cousteau's lucubrations as he and his crew wring every last living drop of pathos out of a sea turtle or a vanishing tribe of Patagonian Indians. Looking at wildlife through a movie camera is a very pale second to seeing it in the flesh, and the fruity music and wordy narrations that usually accompany nature cinematography seems to me the antithesis of their subject. The only nature films that I've liked have been either ones that used natural sounds to give a strong feeling of place (I recall an unforgettable shot of a wolf gnawing on a caribou carcass in a howling blizzard from a National Film Board of Canada documentary) or that used narration to convey genuine information. There haven't been too many of either.

What makes television interesting to me from a natural history viewpoint is much less the nature programs than the odd ecosystem that television as a whole has created. It is a kind of "global village" ecosystem in which biogeographical variations of flora and fauna constantly are being scrambled and rearranged through the ignorance or indifference of technicians. When the medium is the message, the real communicators are not people like Perkins or Cousteau, who are scientists and conservationists as well as television personalities, but the editors, scriptwriters, and producers who control the medium. This can result in ecological incongruities that do strange things to the plots of network programs.

To give one example, there was an episode of *The Waltons* wherein John Boy and his pa go to visit hillbilly relatives deep in the Blue Ridge Mountains of Virginia and find the hillbillys' mountain cabin in a typical California forest of ponderosa pine and manzanita. This environment certainly would have taken Appalachian hill people of the pre-television 1930s by surprise, and it made the relatives' fierce love of their native hills, around which the episode was built, seem even less convincing than most television clichés. In television's cosmopolitan ecosystem, though, a hill is a hill regardless of whether it grows California ponderosa pines or Appalachian tulip trees. Since California's hills are a convenient distance from the Hollywood studios, a kind of ecological imperialism has taken place, with southern California species marching out to conquer the entire televised world—even outer space.

The wren tit is one of the more flagrant ecological imperialists, although one would hardly suspect this from seeing it in the wild. It is a medium-sized grayish-brown songbird that hops about in coastal scrub or chaparral, often with its tail sticking straight up in the air, which is how it gets the "wren" part of its name. The "tit" part comes not from any improper innuendo but from its habit of hanging upside-down to forage for insects or fruits in the manner of bush tits, tiny grayish birds that also inhabit brushy places. The wren tit has a name stuck together from other birds' names because it is an anomalous species without close relatives in North America, and because it is so drab and inconspicuous in its native west coast habitat that not enough people are familiar with it for a common name to have evolved. It is actually a very common bird in California brushlands, easy to see if one waits quietly in the bushes for a few moments, but it still seems an unlikely candidate for world conquest.

If one turns on a television set, however, one is likely to hear the wren tit's easily recognizable "Yip! Yip! Yip! Y-r-r-r-r!" call anywhere from the Rockies to the Himalayas; and I seem to remember birdcalls vaguely like the wren tit's in the hills of Mongo, Merciless Ming's predatory planet in the old Flash Gordon serials. The wren tit has attained this international and possibly interplanetary status simply by singing all year (unlike most birds, which sing mainly during mating season), so that whenever camera crews shoot outdoors in the Hollywood hills, they accidentally pick up wren tit songs as background noise. The fact that such songs are ecologically inappropriate to the Khyber Pass, Scottish Highlands, or other exotic locales is not pertinent to a sound editor. In the global village, a birdcall is a birdcall.

Another incongruous birdcall that is used quite deliberately, on the other hand, is that of a peculiar Australian kingfisher called the kookaburra, or laughing jackass. The kookaburra is peculiar because it hunts on land instead of in rivers like most kingfishers, and because of its outlandish-sounding call. The kookaburra's call is so weird, in fact, that it has been dubbed into just about every jungle film ever made in Hollywood as an obligatory and by now traditional background noise to the sweaty mumblings of jungle explorers, lying in their tents at night, apprehensive of restless natives. Anyone who has watched *Tarzan of the Jungle, Sheena, Queen of the Jungle, Ramar of the Jungle,* or anybody else of the jungle, will recognize the hoot and cackle of the kookaburra's call, which sounds just like its name. Again, the fact that the kookaburra is a daytime bird not found in the jungles of Africa, Asia, or South America is irrelevant to the conventions of television ecology.

It isn't that real jungle nights don't generate sufficiently haunting and bloodcurdling sounds, either. I spent some nights in the Peten lowlands of Guatemala, for example, and didn't miss the kookaburra at all. The earth-shaking roars of howler monkeys; the ghostly, quavering whistles of pauraques (related to our whipporwills); the crackle, whir, and buzz of insects; and a strange, plaintive fluting that might have been the voice of Rima, the bird girl in W. H. Hudson's *Green Mansions,* provided all the tropical ambience one might have wanted. But it's easier for a technician to reach into a tape file marked "jungle noises" than to seek out the real thing, which will be quite different for each particular jungle. So the jungle becomes associated in the minds of millions with a bird that catches lizards and small marsupials in sunny eucalyptus woodlands.

Identifying television birdcalls can be interesting when the medium's message proves not to be. Often calls are played on tape loops as background sound for commercials advertising organic shampoos, whole grain cereals, and other back-to-Eden products. The same call is repeated over and over, so there is plenty of opportunity to recognize it. Mockingbirds seem a favorite of the commercial-makers, for some reason, and I've heard English sparrows, cardinals, robins, California quail, and even hermit thrushes—the best singers of North America—although not much of the thrush's haunting lyricism rubs off on the natural herb protein body enhancing creme under promotion. Birdcalls on regular programs tend to be more accidental and random than on commercials, except when some particular bucolic effect is sought. One thing I wonder about is whether birdcalls on public television BBC programs are any more ecologically appropriate than their Hollywood counterparts. British technicians might be less McLuhanist about rearranging the natural world with their medium, but I don't know enough about British birds to tell.

Birds aren't the only wildlife of the global village, of course. The Pacific treefrog's shrill "creak-it, creak it" call is perhaps just as far flung in the televised universe as the wren tit's, although it's not used as background noise for such a wide range of locations. Television associates frog calls mostly with steamy summer swamps, although the Pacific treefrog does most of its calling in the winter rainy season. (Now that I think of it, I can't recall any specific televised indication that there *is* a winter rainy season in California. Another example of the long arm of the Los Angeles Chamber of Commerce?) The "treet-treet-treet" call of the house cricket is a more appropriate background for summer nights, since it is not confined to the west coast like the Pacific treefrog. It and its generic relatives are found just about worldwide, in fact, which makes them seem very contemporary and media-oriented, although their worldwide distribution is actually an indication of great evolutionary antiquity, crickets having existed in much their present form before the continents drifted apart into their present scattered locations.

I could close this essay with some mournful words about television being prophetic of a new, ecologically impoverished world of modern technology—a world in which wildlife will be as scanty and random as it is on *Charlie's Angels*. The antiquity of the house cricket probably argues against such a conclusion though. The cricket has sung cheerfully through the demise of dinosaurs and wooly mammoths, and I see no reason why it shouldn't continue when the last television aerial is buried under five hundred feet of sedimentary rock. The world has been ecologically impoverished a number of times before, but not so much through the disappearance of small, lowly things such as crickets, frogs, and songbirds as through that of large, dominant things such as dinosaurs, mammoths, and media technicians. An ecosystem as simplified and random as what we see on the networks would easily be stressed to the breaking point. Moreover, it would in all likelihood not be an ecosystem capable of producing something so rich and intricate as a television set.

# Panic and Dream Time

THE god Pan is one of the more incongruous items in the ill-assorted attic of classic mythology. He began as a local nature spirit in Arcadia, a mountainous backwoods area of the Greek Peloponnesus. He is said to have been the god of hunters and shepherds, although the only concrete example of his "worship" I've come across is the practice of beating his statue with squils (a kind of wild onion) when the hunting wasn't going well. According to *The Golden Bough*, this wasn't intended to punish the godlet but to remove any inauspicious influences that might have been interfering with the hunter's luck. Accounts don't say whether the statues thus beaten represented the man-goat of the classical Pan.

Every region of early Greece had its equivalent of Pan, but for some reason the Arcadian contender made it to the big time in Attica sometime during the fifth century B.C. and began a meteoric rise. He is supposed to have appeared to the Athenian ambassadors before the Battle of Marathon and promised to put the invading Persians to flight if they would dedicate a sanctuary to him on the Acropolis. The Persians fled, and Pan got his place on the Acropolis. By the time of the Alexandrian school of philosophy about the first century B.C., Pan was *the* nature god in the Roman Empire; and because his name was synonymous with the Greek word for "all," he was even viewed as a symbol of the universe, an embodiment of the pantheistic religious view that sees God as within nature instead of apart from it. There is a legend that after Christ was born a ship passing the Islands of Echinades heard a mysterious voice cry three times: "When you reach Palodes proclaim that the great god Pan is dead," signifying that the Pantheon was due for replacement by monotheistic Christianity.

Pan's rise may have been based on semantic confusion, though. Scholars now believe that his name was derived not from "pant"—meaning "all"—but from the Indo-European root for the verb "to eat," the same root that resulted in the Latin verb "pascere," meaning "to graze." This does seem a more logical etymology for a god of sheep, goats, and deer. Scholarship hasn't stopped the legend though—nothing seems to stop legends—and Pan lives in the twentieth century as a symbol of nature worship if not an object of worship himself.

I've never been able to figure out exactly what nature worship is supposed to consist of. The words evoke titillating associations of nude romps, satanism, and human sacrifice (*The Wicker Man* being the most recent popular version of these associations) but the reasons that might be behind these pursuits aren't given much attention except for vague references to "fertility." When you think about it, Pan is a distinctly incongruous symbol for nature worship. Half man, half goat? No two species have been as destructive to natural flora and fauna in their combined efforts as *Homo sapiens* and *Capra domesticus*. The goat has prevented more forests than all the agent orange ever manufactured. Tacking parts of a goat onto a symbol of nature worship is a bit like incorporating selections from *Mein Kampf* into the Old Testament.

Other attributes of Pan—the chasing of nymphs and the music of reed pipes—seem more in keeping with the nature god image. Sex is certainly natural, although not necessarily confined to nature worshipers. The sound of wind in reeds (a reed is a large aquatic grass of the genus *Phragmites,* but people are always confusing it with non-grasses such as cattail, rush, and sedge) is one of the loveliest sounds in nature, although I've never heard pan pipes and don't know if they reflect this. I hope they don't sound like the fatuous flute solos they're supposed to sound like.

Pan would be a pretty superficial nature god if his attributes stopped there, but there is another one, his strangest and most convincing. It is his ability to cause an overwhelming and irrational fear—panic—to woodland travelers. This attribute seems much closer to the basic impulse of worship, which is strongly linked with fear as evidenced by the submissive postures that worshipers usually assume. It is as though Pan needed a way of aweing his acolytes into taking him seriously. Not being one of the imposing Olympians, he couldn't do this with bolts from the blue, floods, plagues, or tempests; so he lurked in the underbrush, startling unwary hikers with sudden looks at his face.

I say that the "panic" attribute is the most convincing because it's the only one I've experienced personally, wood nymphs having eluded me to date. Not that your naturalist has ever been seen fleeing through the woods, shrieking in terror, but there have been times in wild places when I've felt my comfortable, normal consciousness—my habitual, educated thought patterns—start to melt around my ears, so to speak. It isn't necessarily an unpleasant sensation, and might be compared to the moving around of dusty metal furniture that can result from metabolization of psychoactive substances. Both experiences can result in intense, traumatic fear—panic—if one is unprepared for them. Both have been used by various cultures as parts of rites of passage, vision quests, and other religious practices. I don't know if some such practices were the origin of the "panic" attribute of this Greek mini-god, but it seems as likely an explanation as any I've seen (particularly since I haven't seen any other explanations).

Not surprisingly, I've had the "panic" sensation most strongly in the wildest place I've been—the St. Elias Mountains in the Yukon Territory. I had hitched up the Alaska Highway to Whitehorse, and was looking for a place to spend a few days in the bush. There was a cabin on my map that looked conveniently close to the Skagway Road, so I set off hitchhiking in that direction on a hot day in June.

For several hours, I encountered nothing except a Canada lynx; then two of the drunkest men I've ever met gave me a ride in a rattletrap pickup. They were having a great time drinking gin from the bottle, and were laughing so hard they could barely sit up. I squeezed into the cab with them, a quantity of spilled tobacco and empty bottles, and a large 30.06 rifle that was leaned negligently against the seat, and we careened off across the muskeg. They offered me gin, and I decided I had better have some to keep up my courage. We were passing some steep road cuts over Dezadeash Lake, and the driver kept veering onto the shoulders.

By the time we came to the place where a jeep trail led off toward the cabin, it was 5 P.M., and I was a little drunk. There were some houses there, and I asked a man if I could stay at the cabin.

"Sure," he said. "It's sixteen miles up there though." I hadn't paid enough attention to the scale of miles on my map, being used to map scales in the lower forty-eight. "And watch out for the grizzly. It chased a jeep for a mile last week."

My chances of survival with the grizzly were clearly much better than they were with the gin drinkers, so I shouldered my pack and set forth despite a sinking sensation in my stomach. Given the time of year, I could probably make it to the cabin before dark—there would only be a few hours of complete night. I may have set some unrecorded record for hiking speed. I sang loudly. When I took off my boots to cross the first of several glacial melt streams I would have to ford, it occurred to me that I now understood exactly what "he was shaking in his boots" meant.

It was a beautiful walk. The trail led through a glacial valley covered with little poplars and a fairy carpet of wildflowers— lupines, paintbrush, forget-me-nots. Marks of civilization vanished after the first half-mile, and all I could see in the distance were the glaciated peaks of the St. Elias, the second-highest range in North America. The rustle of poplar leaves and roar of the stream were the only sounds. As I got farther in, the valley became marshy and the trail climbed along the valley sides. A cow moose and two calves stood in an expanse of rushes, and the elongating Vs of swimming beavers moved across open water. Arctic terns, which spend summers near the Arctic Circle and winters near the Antarctic, circled overhead. From time to time, I passed grizzly tracks and scats. Grizzly signs are considerably more impressive than black bear signs: the tracks are so large and deep you can see every wrinkle of the pads, and the average scat pile would fill a small bucket. There were plenty of black bear signs to compare the grizzly signs with.

As twilight deepened, the pale gray of granite cobbles and poplar trunks became the brightest thing under the sky. A sense of unreality that had begun during the drunken pickup ride also deepened. I began to feel as though I was walking in a dream. There was the feeling that I didn't know quite where I was, that my surroundings might change suddenly as in a dream. The only control I could have over events was to keep walking, and I wasn't altogether sure where that would take me.

I reached the cabin just as it became too dark to walk. A porcupine was sitting on the front porch. I wouldn't have been too surprised if it had opened its mouth and told me to get lost, but it merely grunted and moved aside as might a churlish caretaker. The cabin stood beside a large lake, and I could hear the water lapping on the shore as I tried to sleep. There were no other people about, nor evidence that people had been there recently.

The feeling of being in dream time persisted throughout my stay in the cabin. When I came out on the porch next morning, several snowshoe rabbits were grazing in the grassy clearing around the cabin. They sat up on their hind legs and looked at me, but didn't run away. They stayed in the clearing as I came and went, and I could always look out in the cabin window and see them crouching or sitting up as though listening to sounds I didn't hear. It wasn't behavior I was used to in rabbits, so this too seemed like something in a dream.

Time lost its shape. There was little sense of morning, afternoon, evening, only of long twilights in which I could awaken from sleep and see the rabbits in the clearing, as easily as when I came out the following morning. The sky was often overcast although it didn't rain much, so it was hard to distinguish a cloudy afternoon from a twilit night. Sometimes I'd go into the cabin, shut the door, and read paperback spy thrillers I found there just to get back into linear time for a while.

There was always the grizzly's presence, though I never did encounter it. I kept imagining it coming to the door of the cabin while I went out the window. I walked the boggy slopes scanning every patch of willow, eyeing every ridgetop. I couldn't decide whether I wanted to encounter the grizzly or not. Again, it was like the dreams in which you await something, and only discover if it is a threat or a promise after it has finally appeared.

The grizzly became the same kind of admonitory, mythical figure as the man-goat of the Arcadian mountains—a guardian of the groves and herds, a presence behind the landscape. This leads me to wonder if Pan himself might not have been a pastoralization of an older figure, perhaps one that combined a man and a wild animal instead of a domesticated one. The man-deer "sorcerer" of Lascaux comes to mind. If so, "panic" might be a remnant of a very old kind of consciousness—the "dream time" or "sacred time" that a few Kalahari bushmen and Australian aborigines still inhabit.

My experience in the St. Elias may sound oppressive—it wasn't much "fun"—but it opened up some wide, quiet spaces in my mind. When I left after a week or so, I felt capable of approaching life in general, and human society in particular, from some new angles and with some new energy. Of course, one could say that I was merely relieved to get away from the solitude and the possibility of becoming part of a grizzly scat, but I don't think that would account for the sense of renewal—a sense similar to the renewal one feels on awakening from an awesome and significant dream.

If I'm not being too far-fetched in interpreting "panic" as a remnant of a mytho-poetic consciousness that perpetuated a great deal of harmony between humans and the biosphere, then the Arcadian god may still have something to offer Western civilization. He has the advantage of having been part of it from the beginning. Endemic myths such as Coyote might be more suitable to North America, but Coyote is ultimately the property of

Native Americans, and anyway comes from a time before groves and herds needed "guardians."

Pan is going to have to clean up his act if he hopes to communicate with the modern mind, though. The man-goat might have been significant to pastoral people who understood the inherent wildness of the domestic goat, but it means no more to industrial-urban people than it would have meant to Cro-Magnon reindeer hunters. I'm afraid the quaint veneer of classicism will have to go too—the nymphs, fauns, rustic symphonies. Pan will have to become the patron deity of environmentalists— he makes a much more suitable one than Saint Francis, whose concern for wild things was really very marginal. I have trouble imagining what he will dress himself up as, though. A man-grizzly bear? He would look like one of those circus clowns who stumble about in absurdly oversized trousers, hardly a figure to win devotees. How about a man-bighorn sheep? The bighorn is a powerful but gentle wilderness animal that is not at all destructive in its grazing habits, unlike its domestic cousins. It was John Muir's favorite animal. A man-bighorn sheep would be quite handsome. It would even look a little like a football player, and what could be more attractive to Americans?

# The Nature of Nature Writing

Nature writing is a historically recent literary genre, and, in a quiet way, one of the most revolutionary. It's like a woodland stream that sometimes runs out of sight, buried in sand, but overflows into waterfalls farther downstream. It can be easy to ignore, but it keeps eroding the bedrock.

There is some confusion as to exactly what nature writing is. It usually is associated with essays such as *Walden,* but there is nature fiction, nature poetry, nature reporting, even nature drama, if television documentary narrations are literature. All these have something in common: they are appreciative aesthetic responses to a scientific view of nature, and I think this trait defines the genre. Of course, there was much writing that concerned nature before Linnaeus developed scientific classification in the mid-eighteenth century, but the fascination with nature *itself* that science evoked was new.

Before Linnaeus there were hunting stories, fables, herbals, bestiaries, pastorals, lyrics, and traveler's tales, but nature generally was seen in only two dimensions. It was a backdrop to a historical cosmos, or a veneer over a religious one. Whether it was admired or scorned, the human figure stood in strong relief against it. After Linnaeus began to give even insects impressive Greco-Latinate names, nature rapidly acquired a new substantiality and became a subject as well as a setting. By the 1790s an

English country clergyman who a century or two before might have been writing theological treatises or metaphysical poems produced a book (Gilbert White's *The Natural History of Selborne*) wherein history and religion were interwoven with, sometimes overshadowed by, beech trees and earthworms.

Nature writing has been particularly prevalent in America, for an obvious reason. European colonists found here a world that was for them (if not for the Indians they displaced) empty of historical or religious association. In this world they ignored nature itself at their own risk. The early Jamestown and Boston colonists succeeded in ignoring it to some degree, which perhaps is one reason they clung precariously to the coast for the first hundred years; but by Linnaeus's time, Americans had begun to observe nature closely, and to venture into the wilderness with appreciation.

They observed in a piecemeal fashion at first, and ventured without too much appreciation. Early naturalists, such as Cadwallader Colden and John Bartram, were more interested in extracting rare, valuable plants and animals from the wilderness than in perceiving it as a whole, an attitude in keeping with the Linnaean bias for individual organisms over ecological systems (ecology not having been invented yet). Bartram, a Philadelphia Quaker who collected Venus's-flytraps and other curiosities for wealthy English patrons' gardens, saw the wolves and swamps of the wilderness as uncomfortable obstacles, and his descriptions of Florida and upstate New York in the 1750s and 1760s reflect this. They are robust and accurate, but utilitarian. They are not quite nature writing as we understand it today because an element of poetic sensibility is lacking from their genuine scientific interest.

John's son, William Bartram, supplied the missing element. An artist and dreamer who failed several times at storekeeping and farming, he spent four years alone in the American wilderness and brought poetry to it as decisively as a rather similar figure, Johnny Appleseed, brought fruit. His account of Florida and the southern Appalachians in his book, the *Travels*, is a subtropical escarpment dividing dry Enlightenment from moist Romanticism. William's father had described the waters of one of Florida's celebrated limestone sinkhole springs as smelling "like bilge," tasting "sweetish and loathsome," and boiling up from the bottom "like a pot." Williams saw "an enchanting and amazing crystal fountain, which incessantly threw up, from dark, rocky caverns below, tons of water every minute . . . the blue ether of another world."

If William's effusions have a familiar ring to even the most urban sensibility, there is good reason. After its publication in 1791, Bartram's *Travels* was devoured by the generation of young European poets that included the author of "Kubla Khan." Bartram supplied Coleridge, Wordsworth, Chateaubriand, and others with genuine examples of exotic, Rousseauesque wonders they hungered for—not only "caverns measureless to man," but noble Creek warriors, lovely Cherokee maidens, flowery savannas, fragrant groves, brilliant birds. The wonders seem a little overblown to us today, but they were real, honestly observed, and vividly described. Fragments of their splendor still linger in today's condominium-laden Florida. The "magnificent plains of Alachuah," where Bartram saw "the thundering alligator" and "the sonorous savanna cranes," are now a state preserve, although there's an interstate freeway through one corner of them.

The *Travels* didn't evoke as much interest in America as it did in Europe. Most Americans were unprepared for its glowing picture of wilds that lay only a few days' travel to the west. One reviewer found its subject interesting but its style "disgustingly pompous." As the romantic sensibility filtered westward across the Atlantic, however, Bartram's poetic wilderness followed it. "Do you know Bartram's *Travels*?" Carlyle wrote to Emerson. "Treats of Florida generally, has a wonderful kind of floundering eloquence in it; and has grown immeasurably old. All American libraries ought to provide themselves with that kind of book; and keep them as a future *biblical* article."

If the more flowery passages in Fenimore Cooper's Leatherstocking Tales are to be believed, American pioneers were beginning to sound more like William than his father. In fact, early nineteenth-century frontier letters contain quite a few effusive descriptions of flowery prairies and soaring forests along with more prosaic matters, suggesting that nature-loving in the Romantic mode had caught on.

Nature writing changed as Romanticism evolved into Victorian pragmatic optimism. Its scientific orientation deepened, and at the same time it began to question the directions in which economic applications of science were leading civilization. It became increasingly aware of ecology, in other words. William Bartram hadn't given too much thought to the relationship of civilization and wilderness. (His patron had sent him to scout the Southeast's agricultural and industrial potential as well as to study its natural history.) But Henry Thoreau did, and John Muir after him. Pragmatic, optimistic men (both were mechanically skilled inventors as well as naturalists), they saw wilderness as a remedy for the enervations and constraints of growing industrial towns. They hauled it down from the garret of Romanticism to the Victorian parlor and kitchen. "We require an infusion of hemlock, spruce, or arbor vitae in our tea," wrote Thoreau, with characteristic pungency (and hyperbole). "Hope and the future for me are not in lawns and cultivated fields, not in towns and cities, but in the impervious and quaking swamp."

Although they often are seen as opposed to nineteenth-century expansionism, Thoreau and Muir were men of their time, inhabiting a planet with about a quarter of today's population. Land speculators saw hope and future in quaking swamps too, although they differed from Thoreau in wanting to see them drained after they bought them cheap. One might say that Thoreau and Muir liked the expansive quality of the frontier so much that they wanted to make it permanent, to integrate its challenges and exhilarations with civilization. From this desire, expressed in Thoreau's New England swamp ruminations and Muir's California mountaintop raptures, arose the concept of the wilderness park, America's unique contribution to global culture.

As Victorian optimism ripened into Edwardian euphoria, the words of Thoreau and Muir struck increasingly responsive chords with the public. Expansion of the frontier was making America rich, but it was gobbling up natural resources so fast that the idea of preserving some wilderness for recreation, or at least for future use, had become respectable. Nature writing had a heyday at the turn of the century, especially during the presidency of Theodore Roosevelt, himself a nature writer of sorts. It would be hard to imagine John Muir going camping in Yosemite with the present Republican incumbent, but he did with Teddy Roosevelt. John Burroughs, a less acerbic writer than Thoreau or Muir, enjoyed tremendous popularity with books about countryside wildlife, and went camping with Henry Ford and Thomas Edison as well as Roosevelt.

The heyday didn't survive Muir and Roosevelt. The scientifically conducted carnage of World War I revealed the rot at the Edwardian core, and pragmatic optimism became a mark of naive boosterism. Many American writers were overtaken by a wave of nostalgia for the prescientific, for the nobility in which religion and history can clothe humanity. Muir and Thoreau had complained eloquently of human conceit and destructiveness, but they still had taken for granted a high degree of human significance. It was harder to do this after a generation of young men had been slaughtered in the trenches. The pragmatic remedies of progressives seemed inadequate to modernists, who sought utopias.

The modernist flight of American writers to Europe was a frontier in reverse. Nature writing meant little to its pioneers Pound and Eliot, who turned their backs on Idaho and Missouri to embrace medieval Europe. Even the outdoorsman Ernest Hemingway had a medieval attitude toward wilderness. It was a place for hunting, fishing, or war, not for seeking knowledge, transcendent or otherwise. Knowledge was for priests. D. H. Lawrence excluded Thoreau from his canon of American classics, regarding him as a coldhearted detailer of biotic mechanisms.

But nostalgia for the prescientific degenerated into fascism, helping bring about World War II and even more murderous applications of science. As though seeking an antidote in the serpent that had stung it, the postwar world turned back to pragmatic optimism of a sort, with much talk of new frontiers in the Arctic, the tropics, the oceans, space. Nature writing underwent a resurgence, partly as a result of renewed public uneasiness about its applications. The popularity of Rachel Carson's best-seller *The Sea Around Us,* which eloquently introduced the public to many new discoveries about the biosphere, gave her the time and authority to write *Silent Spring,* which eloquently introduced the public to the many new dangers of pesticides and herbicides.

Carson and other outstanding postwar nature writers, such as Aldo Leopold and Loren Eisely, were somewhat different from their predecessors, reflecting American society's growing dependence on expert knowledge. Bartram, Thoreau, and Muir were amateurs, but Carson, Leopold, and Eiseley were institutionally trained and employed scientists. There were advantages and disadvantages to this. Carson and her colleagues could appeal to vastly expanded knowledge of the biosphere's interdependence when advocating wilderness preservation, whereas Muir and Thoreau worked more from intuition. On the other hand, professional positions may have inhibited postwar writers from the robust partisanship that let John Muir lobby unabashedly for birds and flowers in nineteenth-century Sacramento.

There's no doubt that Carson, Eiseley, and Leopold contributed greatly to the wave of environmental partisanship in the 1960s and 1970s. That surge has encouraged a new crop of nature writers; despite continuing shrinkage of wilderness, there probably are more nature writers today than ever. It remains to be seen whether we'll be as influential as our predecessors. At times the prospects look dim. Since land development became a major industry, there has been an expectation in some quarters that wilderness simply will disappear eventually, replaced by artifice. Some writers seem to have accepted this. They write like undertakers: an elegy on every page. A new book about this or that last wilderness comes out at least once a year.

It's important for us to know how bad things are, but to me there's something unimaginative about the elegists. As dealers in myth, writers ought to know better than to let technocrats and salesmen mesmerize them into believing that civilization can conquer nature. They should understand that this is a myth too, what one might call the myth of nature as loser. But nature is not a loser because it is not a competitor. The nature-as-loser myth was useful when humanity was small and wilderness large; it encouraged the growth of civilization, and of knowledge. It's of doubtful utility to us, who are capable of reducing the biosphere to dust. It is not nature that will have lost in that event.

There's a lot of work for nature writers to do. It's not quite the same work that William Bartram faced. Adventure is a luxury commodity today, packaged by tour agencies. The old, romantic, exotic nature writing is of declining relevance. I wonder how many people have gone to the library to read about something in their local woods and found books about the Arctic, the tropics, the oceans and space, but nothing much about their local woods. I certainly have: it's one more reason I started writing nature books.

Carson, Leopold, and Eiseley did much of their exploring in their studies. The most daunting challenge facing nature writers today is not travel but data. Somebody has to translate information into feelings and visions. This is not to say that nature writers now must spend all their time at computer terminals. Collecting mosquito bites always will go with the job, and there are still more places to do so, even in America, than some people think. They're generally the worse for wear, these places, but they're still alive, still holding up the biosphere, still part of what Wallace Stegner calls "the geography of hope."

# Wetlands in America

Wetlands are subtle things, hard to measure and define. Official estimates of the original wetland acreage in the conterminous United States (the lower forty-eight, that is) have ranged from 127 million to 215 million, or from roughly five to ten percent of wilderness America. That's a very rough estimate indeed, but then the pioneers weren't counting swamps and bogs as they slashed their way west. (Survey marker trees have provided some records, but many species such as elm and ash grow both in swamps and drier places.) Even if they had been counting, they would have had problems because wetlands can change size significantly over relatively short periods, and can be hard to even recognize, as anyone will agree who has started to walk across a meadow and ended up in a bog.

Most people can recognize baldcypress swamps, cattail ponds, or tidal cordgrass marshes, but prairie potholes, sedge meadows, riverbottom forests, vernal pools, pocosins, and fens can be deceptive in dry years, or dry times of year, although they are well-documented wetland types. To the casual eye, most wetland trees, shrubs, and herbs aren't markedly different from dry land counterparts, and even such wetland peculiarities as the carnivorous sundews and bladderworts aren't particularly eye-catching. What's more, many places that aren't well-documented as wetland can get pretty wet at times.

I once worked for an Ohio regional park agency that presided over a collection of old fields, woodlots, and ravines snatched from the jaws of suburbia, pretty places, but with nothing legendary about them in the way of swamps. Certainly, none of the parks were *called* swamps. The administration shied away from such buggy connotations, preferring titles like "woods," "creek," or, as a last resort, "ponds." I doubt if the parks bulked large in any official wetland estimates. Apart from a few buttonbush pools and creek oxbows, they just weren't very wet for most of the year, just nice tidy woods and fields for suburban strolls.

Then the March rains thawed the ground and filled thousands of unnoticed little holes and channels. Suddenly, the parks were making up for the previous twelve months' tameness by reenacting all the invertebrate and herpetological unruliness of the past billion years. Quiet glades became raucous chorus frog and spring peeper bathhouses, salamander spermatophores littered pool bottoms like discarded shreds of plastic bags, a yard-long snapping turtle gobbled fairy shrimp in an oxbow festooned with egg masses, gray flatworms picked at an orange crayfish carcass. An entire swamp ecosystem had surfaced, as though the ground had dissolved and let up the creepers and crawlers from some prehistoric realm out of Jules Verne.

Of course, they'd simply been there through the dry months, waiting. Such is the nature of our watery biosphere that any healthy bit of terrain will develop wetland attributes with surprising speed given the opportunity. In a sense, the term "dry land" is a misnomer, a phantasm of the dualistic mind. Land and water are not opposites but complements. Land so thoroughly compacted and drained as to be without water is no longer land: it is pavement, or dust.

One could say that most of primeval North America was wetland, at some times, in some ways, even the desert, where cloudburst pools that may fill the flats once in a decade promptly produce fairy shrimp and spadefoot toads. A certain degree of wetland is normal wherever water is allowed to seek its unobstructed way and find its undepleted level. I've never been in a wilderness area where wetland wasn't a theme repeated with variations many times in a day's walk by springs, seeps, wet meadows, lake margins, floodplains, fault slips, hanging bogs, sinkholes. The pioneers encountered the theme even more frequently, with delight at the abundance of good springs, with terror at the engulfment of wagons and oxen, as they penetrated a vast hydrological system about whose intricacies we now can only guess, having largely destroyed it with our ditches, canals, levees, sewers, wells, and reservoirs.

Enough remains of the system for us to have a crude understanding of it. The most recent, Wisconsinan glaciation largely caused it, directly or indirectly. By leaving behind great drifts of undulating, pocked, silty, or otherwise water-retaining terrain as it melted, glaciation directly caused the bogs and fens of New England, the Upper Midwest, and the Western mountains, as well as the swamp forests of the Great Lakes and the prairie potholes of the Northern Plains. It created the intermountain marshes of the West just about as directly as alpine glaciers melted into valley lakes, which then silted up.

Glaciation indirectly created coastal marshes and mangrove swamps by raising ocean levels as it melted; there were tidal wetlands before the ice sheet receded, but they now lie far offshore. Similarly, glaciation helped create the great bottomland swamps of the southeast as fluctuating ocean levels and floods of river-borne meltwater changed drainage patterns. Even desert wetlands aren't free of glacial influence, since many depend on fossil aquifers left over from glacier-forming pluvial periods. Most wetland plants and animals had been on the continent for millions of years before the Wisconsinan glaciation, however, and they reclaimed the soggy barrens it left behind in a geological instant.

Marching northward in the glacier's wake came much the same wetland ecosystems we have today, minus the odd mastodon or ground sloth: first tundra with its masses of ground-nesting birds among the tussocks and cotton sedges; then the spruce, larch, and poplar bogs of the taiga, home of the stilt-legged, pondweed-eating moose; then northern deciduous elm, ash, and maple swamps, where lived the almost equally aquatic elk; and finally southern deciduous tupelo, gum, and baldcypress swamps, home of that most ancient of wetland creatures, the alligator, effectively unchanged since the pre-dinosaur Triassic Period. Moving from east to west, the post-glacial observer would have seen an even wider wetland transect, from Atlantic cordgrass marshes, to white cedar swamps, to sycamore and cottonwood floodplains, to seasonally-flooded canebrakes and tallgrass prairies where the buffalo soggily roamed, to reed-hidden, swan-haunted potholes, to sweetwater marshes at the base of the Rockies, to increasingly bitter and salty marshes in the Great Basin sinks, to tule marshes and alder swamps beyond the Sierra and Cascades, and finally to Pacific cordgrass and pickleweed marshes.

Such transects are mere abstracts of living complexity and diversity, of course. Not only do they inadequately describe common wetlands, they slight the fascinating rarities and oddities: the crocodiles at the tip of Florida, the pupfish thriving in ninety-degree waters of desert oases, the blind minnows and salamanders of subterranean wetlands, the cobra plants and endemic wildflowers of the Pacific Coast's deceptively barren-looking serpentine wetlands, the glacial relict wetlands still sprinkled over the north temperate belt where buried blocks of the glacier planted them, natural refrigerators for spruce and arborvitae, botanical time machines concealing paleontological clocks in their pollen layers, mammoth bones and mammoth-hunter spearheads in their peat deposits.

Some of these, puddles high on mountains or deep in caves, may not seem like wetlands at all. Yet for me it is not so much the location or extent of a wetland that defines the phenomenon as a certain fecund interface of air, water, and soil, and a single puddle can provide that as well as a thousand. I don't think it's possible to overestimate the importance to evolutionary life of that interface. It's likely that life first appeared in shallow waters enriched by dissolved minerals and warmed by sunlight, and if it didn't, it quickly moved there, as various wriggle marks in Paleozoic mudflats indicate. Since then, the development of land as we know it has been to a great extent a product of interaction between living wetlands and various geological and climatic forces. Mountains erode into floodplain swamps and delta marshes, which fossilize into sandstone and shale and then are uplifted into new mountains. Certainly, the mountain-leveling force of industrial civilization would not have evolved without the fossil swamps of the coal measures.

Fifteen thousand years of postglacial swamps and marshes prepared a North American continent eminently suited to agro-industrial exploitation, which has always seemed a little uncanny and ironic to me. Such a resource accumulation, all that lake and river water to pollute, all that topsoil and groundwater to deplete, seems to hint at some not-very-healthy divine intervention: land as a piggy bank left under a pillow by an overindulgent parent. Of course, the pioneers didn't perceive the trackless, howling Dismals and Limberlosts into which history shoved them as a porcelain indulgence, but they broke them just the same, and we've been spending them ever since.

A television mini-series might be made of the saga of swamp exploitation in America, one of those dynastic epics that carry a large, colorful cast from the squabbles and philanderings of the Colonies to the squabbles and philanderings of the present. It would concern, say, the Fenimans, a Puritan family down on their luck for some entertainingly scandalous reason who come to Massachusetts Bay Colony and raise cattle on the salt marshes. The Fenimans don't know that salt marsh cordgrasses are four times as productive as twentieth-century cornfields will be, but they have a sharp eye for the produce—maybe a little too sharp for their neighbors, whose complaints about numerous, wide-ranging Feniman cattle add a lively note of conflict to early episodes. Conflict doesn't daunt the Fenimans: they raise large hay barns, and larger families.

The salt marshes get a little trampled and eroded after the first century, and the Fenimans move on. A particularly fetching daughter marries into the wealthy Reed family, which is developing rice, indigo, and sugar plantations in the black rush marshes behind South Carolina barrier islands. A particularly imaginative son flees some trouble with church elders and becomes an Indian trader in western Pennsylvania, enriching himself on the proceeds of beaver ponds. Less imaginative sons move stolidly but steadily west across New England, pasturing stock in sedge meadows, draining bogs, planting bottomland.

The tempo quickens as the French and Indian War is fought over the beaver supply, and the clever son gets even richer than before. The fetching daughter produces another imaginative scion who moves south to Florida with an exotic, unruly collection of slaves and starts a sugar plantation near the mouth of the St. Johns River, where the slaves almost revolt at being forced to eat too many ducks, oysters, and other cheap foods. The stolid sons keep pushing west, fanning out, some north to even boggier Vermont and New Hampshire, some to the hardwood and cedar swamps of Pennsylvania and New York, some south to Virginia tupelos and sweetgums. One loops back to the New Jersey salt marshes, as yet less trampled than the New England ones.

Then disasters strike. The fur trader chooses the wrong side in the Revolution, and is lynched by a patriotic mob. His son has to go to work as a trapper for the Hudson Bay Company, and disappears into the vast, soggy forests beyond the Great Lakes. Stolid sons are struck down right and left by Hessian bullets, Mohawk arrows, epidemics: the New Jersey branch is completely terminated by the yellow fever outbreak of 1793. Sequestered from the war, the Florida son lives to a ripe old age, but the Seminoles burn him out in 1835, and he dies of apoplexy.

Things improve after that. Manifest Destiny is underway, and the Fenimans find swamps that make the sandy Atlantic shore seem miserly. The Reeds move to the Mississippi bottomlands and get rich beyond their wildest dreams on the accumulated silt of half a continent. Stolid Feniman sons prosper more modestly as they pour west from the Appalachian crest, through the Ohio River bottoms, and into the blackland wet prairies and lake muck swamps of Ohio, Indiana, and Illinois. These roosts of the passenger pigeon and haunts of the muskelunge disappear into drains and ditches almost faster than the historian can record as demographic momentum carries more Fenimans across the Mississippi to the less level but equally damp and rich moraines of Iowa, Wisconsin, Minnesota, and the Dakotas, where they encounter the fur trader's heir, who has established a post of his own on the Missouri, and gets his furs from the Bear River marshes and the Wilamette Valley.

Prosperity is never unbroken, or there would be no sagas. War strikes again, and Union troops sack the Reed plantations, turning their most valuable assets into American citizens. Dispossessed sons drift west and pick up odd jobs along the Louisiana and Texas coasts, fishing, trapping, cypress lumbering. A Blackfoot war party terminates the Feniman fur-trading branch. Most of the stolid Fenimans return from the Civil War intact, on the other hand, and since the high, dry plains beyond the pothole country offer little enticement to the unimaginative, they tend to stay home more than their fathers had. This is not always a joy to fathers faced with dividing up homesteads, but they get along more or less comfortably for the next half-century, between depressions, droughts, and floods. There are more droughts and floods as more Fenimans install more tiles, plow more bluestem and bulrush, and cut more bur oaks, but this is ascribed to the fecklessness of the younger generation, not the niceties of soil drainage.

Things are a bit more colorful with the Reeds, many of whom have sunk to bayou shacks. The imaginative gene shows up again in one Texas son, who parlays some sharp practices in cattle and plume dealing into a muddy tract of huisache and mesquite along the lower Rio Grande. By the turn of the century, steam technology has helped him transform it into a booming supplier of urban markets hungry for citrus and fresh winter vegetables.

War is not always a misfortune for Fenimans and Reeds, especially if it happens someplace else. The farm boom of World War I encourages both to expand, meaning more cabbages and corn, fewer wood ducks and black-bellied tree ducks. Farm prices dip in favor of commerce and speculation in the twenties, but the Fenimans ride the decade out comfortably enough, waiting for the good times to trickle down, which perhaps is why few are prepared for the thirties. Drought and depression hit them hard: they have a tradition of leaving land for better places, but not of land leaving them in dust clouds or county auctions. The experience is traumatic, and the number of Fenimans farming former wetlands in North America begins to decline for the first time in three centuries.

Most drift into midwestern commerce or industry and soon regain a modest comfort. The imaginative gene shows up yet again as one son, tractored out of a South Dakota farm, hitchhikes to California and gets a job on the dredge in the San Joaquin delta. After serving in the Seabees in World War II, he moves to the Bay Area, contracts with some landowners, and starts building G.I. Bill housing on fill. By 1985, he is the richest Feniman who ever lived, with a million-dollar second home overlooking the salt marshes of Stinson Beach.

The sprawling Feniman saga would be lent a certain elegance by its hourglass plot, starting with a few Fenimans and thousands of wetland acres and ending with thousands of Fenimans and a few wetland acres, perhaps none. The salt marshes would have become city dumps and sewage plants, the bogs and sedge meadows would be reservoirs and resorts, the black rush marshes golf courses and retirement communities, the wet prairies soybean fields, the Mississippi floodplains the same, the Rio Grande lagunas a suburb of Brownsville, the San Joaquin tule marshes cotton fields and alkaline settling ponds.

Yet reality is less elegant than dynastic sagas. Millions of Americans might be content to see every wetland acre converted to inheritable currency (twenty-eight percent of respondents of a 1979 Florida survey thought wetlands more nuisance than value), but millions of wetland acres remain. It's hard to say how many. Not only are we vague about the original amount and confused about the definition, wetlands are diminishing so rapidly that this year's total may have little relation to last year's. It's probably fair to say that the conterminous United States had lost well over a third of its wetlands by 1950, and that, at a yearly loss rate of between 380,000 and 450,000 acres since then, it has now lost over half. The Fish and Wildlife Service's 1984 *National Wetlands Inventory* estimates that fifty-four percent had gone by the mid-1970s, so depending on one's preferred estimate of the original, we now have between ninety and forty million acres left. That may seem like a lot of swamp, but figures don't address the quality factor. In 1957, wetland biologist Paul Errington maintained that less than a quarter of the original acreage remained fit for waterfowl.

Wetlands persist in America for two reasons. The more historically important one is that they can be difficult and expensive to destroy. My favorite swamp story is the one about the elderly ex-slave who worked on Captain Henry Jackson's dredge when Jackson was trying to drain the east part of the Okefenokee into the St. Mary's River. The old man is supposed to have been the first to ask why Jackson's canal water was flowing west into the swamp instead of east into the river, a nice variant on The Emperor's New Clothes. Jackson died after dredging only twelve of the estimated three hundred miles of canals required to drain the Okefenokee, and it took him seven years to do that. It would have been a temporary blessing to local Fenimans even if he'd succeeded, since the Okefenokee is a giant peat bog on white sand, and its "reclaimed" soils would have succumbed to fire, erosion, and southern heat even faster than the Everglades' limestone-based mucks. Wiser successors, the Hebard Cypress Company, built tracks on pilings, skimmed off the big timber, and left the swamp to the waterfowl, the alligator poachers, and the New Deal.

The second reason has arrived late, but is presently the most important one, and likely to remain so. Some people value wetlands for qualities other than cropland or building potential, an esteem that has grown less quickly and conspicuously than love of forests, mountains, or even deserts, but still has deep, if eccentric, historical roots. William Bartram, the sometimes neglected grandfather of American wilderness appreciation, showed a virtually unqualified admiration for eighteenth-century Georgia and Florida swamps, although he had to endure fevers, hurricanes, and twenty-foot alligators in them. "What a beautiful retreat is here!" he wrote of the St. Johns River country, a remnant of which is preserved in Florida's Lake Woodruff National Wildlife Refuge, "blessed unviolated spot of earth. . . . What a beautiful display of vegetation is here before me! seemingly unlimited in extent and variety."

Bartram also displayed a classic case of the schizophrenia that can afflict wilderness lovers in societies largely indifferent to their enthusiasm. After devoting some exhilarated passages to the Appalachicola River bottoms, "the most extensive Cane-break that is to be seen on the face of the whole earth . . . the most magnificent amphitheatre or circus perhaps in the whole world," he proceeded dutifully to state the obvious: "Under the culture of industrious planters and mechanics . . . almost every desirable thing in life might be produced and made plentiful here. . . . Corn, Rice, Indigo, Sugar-cane, Flax, Cotton, Silk, Cochineal, and all the various esculent vegetables."

Fifty years later, John James Audubon wasn't even schizophrenic about Florida swamps and their discomforts. "I have been deceived most shamefully about the Floridas," he wrote, "scarcely a bird is to be seen, and those of the most common sort . . . the eternal labyrinth of waters and marshes, interlocked and apparently never-ending, the whole surrounded by interminable swamp—all these things have a tendency to depress my spirits."

Between schizophrenia and depression, American swamp preservation got a wobbly start and advanced haltingly. In 1853 Thoreau might proclaim "my temple is the swamp," but in 1869 John Muir would get "tangled . . . like a fly in a spider web" as he tried to walk across "thorny, watery" Florida, and would nearly die of malaria. The specter of fever haunted every nineteenth- and early twentieth-century naturalist. Mary Austin walked around the Mojave Desert with aplomb, but when it came to the marshes west of the Sierra, she showed a shrewd faint-heartedness. "Last and inevitable resort of overflow is the tulares, great wastes of reeds . . . in sickly, slow streams. The reeds, called tules, are ghostly pale in winter, in summer deep poisonous-looking green, the waters thick and brown, the reed beds breaking into dingy pools, clumps of rotting willows. . . . The tulares are full of mystery and malaria. That is why we have meant to explore them and have never done so."

Such ambivalence made the righteousness that worked so well for Muir in the Sierra difficult to tap in the cause of swamps. While Yosemite and Yellowstone were drawing nationwide admiration and protection, state legislatures were selling off the Okefenokee and Everglades at prices like 26.5 cents an acre. The federal government had virtually abdicated any authority over wetlands, first through Chief Justice Roger Taney's decision that submerged lands beneath navigable waters were state property, then by simply giving away huge tracts in the Swamp Lands acts of 1849, 1850 and 1860. The Sidney Laniers and Gene Stratton Porters could write movingly of wetland loveliness, but somehow it wasn't awesome or substantial enough for nineteenth-century preservationist instincts, obsessed with cliffs and geysers.

People finally began protecting swamps not for the swamps' sake, but for what was in them. Audubon may have found little of interest in Florida's "eternal labyrinth", but later ornithologists found much, and the first effective wildlife preservation movement coalesced around the slaughter of egrets and other wading birds by the turn-of-the-century plume trade. A realization that the birds' rookeries and feeing grounds would have to be protected as well as their hides led to the first swamp preserves as the Audubon Society began leasing and patrolling cypress strands and mangrove hells.

A much bigger group of wetland birds, with a much bigger group of admirers, also was wearing thin at the turn of the century. From the humblest farm boy to President Theodore Roosevelt, American sportsmen had grown up to view almost unlimited waterfowl bags as a birthright, and it must have seemed like subversion when the flocks began to dwindle. Yet it couldn't be blamed on anarchists, or even market hunters; the evidence was too concretely there in the duck club photographs festooned with feathered carcasses and in the ditches and culverts that increasingly defined the countryside. Such considerations must have been in Roosevelt's mind when he established the first national wildlife refuge in 1903, although that was a seashore rookery rather than a duck marsh. Duck marshes looked too much like potential homesteads in 1903, so Teddy spoke softly.

The next two decades saw progress toward wetland preservation as well as accelerating wetland destruction. Francis Harper, naturalist and Bartram scholar, thoroughly explored the Okefenokee and brought it public attention in books. Another unassuming explorer, landscape architect Ernest F. Coe, did the same for the Everglades by tirelessly lobbying for preservation. Will Dilg, founder of the Izaak Walton League, was one of the first to perceive the vital relationship between wetlands and water quality, and promoted the first big wetland national wildlife refuge, the Upper Mississippi. The man who probably did the most for wetlands in the twenties was duck-hunting newspaper cartoonist J. N. "Ding" Darling, whose drawings of trampled potholes ringed with blazing shotguns must have been worth thousands of words.

The federal government had gotten back into the wetlands game with the Rivers and Harbors Act of 1899, but not for the sake of preservation. On the contrary, the job of ditching and dredging had proved too much for the private and local sectors, so the pork barrel began its ponderous roll, throwing up levees, spoil banks, and dams in its wake. With presidents who equated government with business interests, with the Corps of Engineers drowning swamps along navigable waters and the Bureau of Reclamation draining them inland, there was little enough wetland conservation, much less preservation, at the federal level.

Even Ding Darling's popularity probably wouldn't have prompted much federal action for wetlands if the financial bubbles of the twenties hadn't burst, dropping land prices and discouraging speculators. As drought dust settled in fiscally stagnant air, new things happened. The Migratory Bird Conservation Act of 1929 and the Migratory Bird Hunting and Conservation Act of 1934 provided funds through congressional authorization and duck stamp sales for buying back some of the wetlands the government had previously given away. Most of these were duck marshes, as was to be expected, but not all.

The U.S. Biological Survey, the beginning of today's U.S. Fish and Wildlife Service, our main wetland manager, started out emphasizing the economically productive aspect of its acquisitions (the Fish and Wildlife Service still emphasizes it), but its mandate was not really that simple, fortunately. A new specter had risen from the swamps by the Depression. Extinction may not be as frightening in the short run as malaria, but its implications are not unlike those of a deadly, wasting disease. The passenger pigeon and Carolina parakeet were already extinct in the twenties, but it had still been possible to imagine them surviving in remote swamps. These were, or seemed, the wildest remaining places, and they did contain other frontier echoes—whooping cranes, ivory-billed woodpeckers, limpkins, Everglades kites, Audubon's caracaras, Bachman's warblers. The twenties were the last gasp of romantic expansionist euphoria, however (as opposed to today's hard-eyed variety), and the Depression's gritty dawn seems to have prompted a general, if tacit, recognition that there wasn't much left to find in swamps, but a great deal to lose. It is hard otherwise to account for the sudden public willingness to save places like the Everglades and Okefenokee, both of which were authorized for federal protection in the thirties.

The people didn't save enough. If the public sector had protected northeastern Louisiana's 120-square-mile Singer Tract of Tensas River bottomlands in 1934, an area less than one-fifth the size of the Okefenokee, we might now have descendants of the estimated seven pairs of ivorybills that lived in the tract then, along with panthers, red wolves, and Bachman's warblers. Unlike the Okefenokee, the Singer Tract still contained much valuable timber, and by 1943 the ivorybills were gone along with the "overmature" trees they depended on for their borer beetle diet staple.

A lot more than ivory-billed woodpeckers was gone or going in the 1940s and 1950s. Errington considered this the major period of prairie pothole destruction. In 1949–50 alone, 188,000 acres were drained with federal assistance in Minnesota and the Dakotas, countless more privately. Duck populations were down to a third of their nineteenth-century numbers that year. By the 1960s, Iowa and Illinois wetlands were ninety-five percent drained, and Great Lakes marshes had declined by seventy-one percent. Most wetlands with agricultural potential had fared about the same. California's once vast valley wetlands were ninety percent reduced, and southern Florida, alternately parched and drowned by a century of ditching and by vast Army Corps flood control and reclamation projects begun in 1947, had lost ninety percent of its wading birds in a generation. Coastal marshes suffered almost as badly from navigation channel dredging and filling and urban sprawl. Long Island lost thirty percent of its marshes in the decade from 1954 to 1964.

DDT and other persistent biocides entered the picture in the forties and fifties, with results that seem predictable in hindsight. Wetlands not only were sprayed for mosquito control but received poisoned runoff from uplands and towns. After twenty years, Long Island marsh soil contained thirteen pounds of DDT per acre. Populations not only of eagles, ospreys, and waterfowl but of fish, shrimp, and crabs declined. The pesticides combined with more traditional effluviums such as sewage, heavy metals, and waste petrochemicals to produce corrosive wastelands like the Hackensack marshes I recall from childhood, wherein the stench made breathing difficult.

Yet pollution may have helped teach us a lesson. In its insidious way, striking quietly at the bases of food pyramids as well as the tops, it demonstrated that wetlands must be valued for healthy muck—bacteria, algae, dead grass—as well as for ducks, since muck makes ducks. It demonstrated that wetlands must be valued for themselves. As ecologists such as Errington and the Odums began paying close attention to the inner workings of muck, they found some unexpected things: not only that salt marshes are more productive than cornfields but that floodplain forests are efficient regulators of stream flow, that swamps store water with less evaporation loss than reservoirs, that marshes purify wastewater, that most commercial and sport seafoods breed not in the sea but in tidal marshes and estuaries, where their fry and larvae feed on cordgrass detritus, that is, on muck.

Weighty discoveries, but they did not sink quickly into the complacent Jello of postwar prosperity. *Silent Spring* may have been a bestseller in 1962, but Congress took a decade more to pass, much less enforce, significant pesticide control and water quality legislation. Luckily for some wetlands, postwar prosperity wasn't expressed only in home and car sales. People wanted places to go in their new cars, and it was getting harder to find them as home sales soared. Even boggy open space looked good to a generation that had grown up without traditional fears of fevers and miasmas, so swamps finally got firmly, if quietly, hitched to the recreation bandwagon. Public pressure forced a reorganization of the Duck Stamp program to increase land acquisition in 1958, and even more importantly, the Outdoor Recreation Resources Review Commission was established. It was the Commission's 1962 report, *Outdoor Recreation in America,* that prompted the creation in 1965 of the Land and Water Conservation Fund, which probably has done more to perpetuate local wetland preservation than any other public institution. When I worked for the Ohio park agency, Land and Water Conservation matching funds helped it acquire the only remaining pothole marsh complex in the area, and the only relatively pristine, undammed floodplain.

Wetland preservation underwent a modest heyday in the 1970s, when the Land and Water Conservation Fund tripled in five years, the Fish and Wildlife Service made plans to acquire an additional 1.9 million acres to keep waterfowl populations at historical levels, and an American president came right out and said, "The Federal Government will no longer subsidize the destruction of wetlands." Even privately-owned wetlands got a boost from Section 404 of the Federal Water Pollution Control Act Amendments of 1972, which required the Army Corps of Engineers to start regulating filling of wetlands shoreward from established harbor lines (a subsequent court decision widened federal authority to include all U.S. waters).

Wetlands finally joined canyons and mountains in becoming the subjects of nationwide preservation campaigns. The Everglades and adjacent Big Cypress swamps escaped conversion into a jetport and sacrifice area for Greater Miami, and central Florida wetlands were not gutted by a barge canal. The Big Cypress became a 570,00 acre national preserve, and other stretches of cypress, sawgrass, mangrove, cordgrass, leatherleaf, and pitcher plant became not only parks and wildlife refuges but wilderness areas as well, inaccessible not only to dredges and draglines, but to outboards and airboats.

Nobody knows how much wetland there is under wilderness designation because the managing agencies haven't tried to count it. Any wilderness is likely to contain wetland, as I've said; but since the wilderness preservation system encompasses only two percent of the conterminous United States, the designated acreage certainly is small in proportion to the original, or even the remnant. It also is concentrated in agriculturally marginal areas such as the sandy southeastern coastal plain and the granitic Boundary Waters; and there are problems even with that, since fishermen can get just as passionate about outboards as hunters can about ORVs. The country's biggest freshwater swamp, the Atchafalaya, has no designated wilderness, nor do the remnants of many other once-vast morasses—California tulares, prairie riverbottoms, midwestern lake plains.

Rather surprisingly for a statistic-loving civilization, nobody knows how much wetland there is in *any* protected form, wilderness or otherwise. The Forest Service, Bureau of Land Management, and National Park Service all manage substantial wetland acreage; but only the Fish and Wildlife Service has attempted to quantify its holdings, and it appears to have doubts about those. Its 1977 *Proceedings of the National Wetland Protection Symposium* cited twelve million acres of FWS controlled wetlands in the conterminous United States but its 1984 *National Wetlands Inventory* seemed to cite only seven million (with an additional twenty-nine million in Alaska). If our ignorance of federal wetland is deep, our ignorance of state, local, and private is abysmal. Few conservation bodies at those levels count their wetlands either, and who would put the figures together if they did? They tend, furthermore, to get tangled up in federal programs because so many local projects have been pursued with matching funds.

Of course, the 1970s weren't any millenium for wetlands, which continued disappearing as rapidly as ever, succumbing to soybean culture, peat or phosphate mining, monoculture forestry, condominium development, and other economic fads. The Mississippi Basin states indulged in a veritable orgy of soybeans during the farm price boom, and reduced their bottomland forests to five (or three) million of an original twenty-four (or twenty-five) million acres. Timber companies converted a half-million acres of North Carolina pocosins (elevated shrub bogs specializing in Venus flytraps) to large-scale agriculture. Urban expansion in northern and central Florida shrank wetlands so drastically that the climate seems to have become cooler and drier. The Sunbelt boom also stressed southwestern riparian ecosystems already troubled by irrigation and grazing. Despite brave words, the Carter administration did not stop federal subsidization of wetland destruction: the Garrison Diversion project of North Dakota and other boondoggles shamble on.

Unfortunately the seventies seem a little like the light at the beginning of the tunnel now. The federal role in wetland preservation has declined since 1980, to say the least, although not as drastically as James Watt promised when he put a moratorium on further acquisitions for refuges and parks, attempted to develop refuges, and tried to use park acquisition funds for park construction projects. Subsequent interior secretaries have been more circumspect about niggardly acquisition and management budgets, but the budgets haven't been much better than Watt's, and would have had a similar effect if Congress hadn't increased them by factors that seem enormous in comparison (anything seems enormous in comparison to nothing) but are modest by 1970s standards.

The acquisition slowdown has been complemented, of course, by the regulatory slowdown. Although environmentalists beat back the Gorsuch/Burford EPA and the Corps of Engineers' 1982 attempt to abdicate its wetland responsibilities, generally sluggish and lenient administrative attitudes have not been lost on developers; and if causes get buried in piles of documents, effects are becoming increasingly visible. I've noticed more malls and condos sprouting on San Francisco Bay fill in the past couple of years than in the previous decade. After surviving a power plant and a refinery, the endangered salt marsh harvest mouse is once again under attack, by a golf course this time, and oil companies continue illegal discharges into Bay wetlands.

The scattered, often inconspicuous or evanescent character of wetlands makes the effects of the Reagan slow-down hard to calculate. There still are fewer big-name wetlands than canyons or mountains, and wild places that don't make good copy are easy to whittle away. While Watt's attempt to cut off authorized funds for Big Cypress Preserve was decried, square miles of Gulf Coast bottomland silently became soybean fields and housing tracts. We hear about them later, when denuded rivers flood out new property owners.

In the end the Reagan administration won't be judged for what it did—its petty squeezing of nickel-and-dime budgets, its Scrooge-like withholding of authorized funds—but for what it didn't do. After the wide public acceptance of an environmental agenda in the seventies, an eighties administration had a chance to save, or even restore, significant samples of neglected wild ecosystems. Read what Fish and Wildlife Biologist Brooke Meanley had to say in 1972 about the Arkansas River bottomlands downstream from a place called Arkansas Post: "When I went to that area, I always had the feeling that I had stepped back two centuries into the past. There was a sense of wildness there that I never felt in the heart of the Okefenokee, the Great Dismal Swamp, or the Everglades." It seems doubtful now that future Americans will be able to share that feeling in that place.

A lot of credit is due private and local conservation bodies for attempts to fill the federal vacuum. With a little tax-deductible help from industry, the Nature Conservancy has initiated effective programs to acquire wetlands in southeastern river bottoms, migratory waterfowl flyways, Atlantic barrier islands, and western deserts. An estimated half of Conservancy projects are water-related. Under Governor Bob Graham, the state of Florida has begun a bold attempt to reverse some of the damage done to its hydrological system in the past forty years. The "Save our Everglades" program has prevailed upon the Corps of Engineers to plug some of the ditches that drain life from the national park's borders, and proposes to acquire large wetland acreage for protection and to rebuild Alligator Alley and the Tamiami Trail to increase southward water flow and reduce wildlife mortality. Graham has said the program means "to provide that by the year 2000 the Everglades will look and function more as it did in 1900 than it does today," which somebody had to say if the Everglades was not to continue deteriorating into a dried-out, pantherless stretch of Brazilian pepper.

Only Washington can make the Florida program work, however. The water management system that is strangling the Everglades is congressionally mandated, and only congressional action can change it significantly. Local and private conservation can't obviate the fact that North America is subject to one of the most powerful central governments in history. If that government chooses to neglect air and water quality in favor of Star Wars technology, not even the most carefully managed duck marsh in the remotest county in the most environmentally conscious state will escape the consequences of those choices. If groundwater pollution doesn't get it, acid rain will. No swamp is an island.

Fortunately for those making the choices, the consequences won't become clear until the last acre of exploitable wetland is filled, drained, or poisoned in the mid-to-late twenty-first century. Wetlands are less dramatic in their destruction than forests or rivers. They tend to die by inches, a peat fire here, a fish die-off there, an oxidation failure here, and they may continue to provide wetland benefits such as streamflow regulation or groundwater retention long after they have ceased to be complete, or even discernible, wetland ecosystems. After the cattails and rushes have been plowed up, the spongy peat persists. Only when the apparently dry land is committed to "highest" use, to pavement and foundations, do the benefits finally stop, and then they may stop fast, with the speed of flood or wildfire.

It will be a chancy experiment, this replacement of a system that has persisted since the Paleozoic Era, this revolution from land to pavement. Failure will be accompanied by human suffering on a large scale. We can get an inkling of that scale by considering the history of China, which has (or had) ecosystems eerily similar to ours: glaciated mountains and grasslands releasing heavy silt loads into rivers that then flow down through vast, soggy plains. China has (or had) the only other alligator species in the world. Long ago, the Chinese valleys were deforested, and the rivers were confined by levees and canals administered by a strong central government. Without broad, forested floodplains to disperse over, silt built up in the river beds, raising them above valley level. When levees failed, as they did when the central government failed, the rivers flooded so powerfully that they sometimes changed course over hundreds of miles. One such flood, of the Yellow River in 1931, killed 3.7 million people.

Of course, that was before modern engineering. China is harnessing her rivers with concrete now, just as we have, and harnessed rivers can't do such things, can they? Consider the Mississippi where it strains at the Army Corps of Engineer's Old River Control Structure that keeps it flowing toward Baton

Rouge and New Orleans instead of flooding into the Atchafalaya Basin, population 140,000. The river emptied into Atchafalaya Bay once, and it appears to have decided to do so again—pretty soon, probably. Silt is no great respecter of high technology, accumulating impartially behind dirt or steel-reinforced concrete.

Population growth is the generally accepted cause of such predicaments, but I think they are as much rooted in perception as history. Land and water are not really separate things, but they are separate words, and we perceive through words. We see a river as a separate from its swampy floodplain, but the floodplain sycamores and cottonwoods are ecologically as much a part of the river as its deepest channels. The cordgrass marsh is part of the estuary, the cypress bay is part of the lake, the pothole marsh part of the cornfield, the leatherleaf bog part of the cow pasture. We need a wider vision of things, and we don't have to go to outer space to get it. Goethe provided one two centuries ago when he showed us greedy altruist Faust draining tidal marshes with demonic helpers, displacing elderly cottagers in the process:

> Human sacrifices bled,
> Tortured yells would pierce the night
> And where the blazes seaward sped,
> A canal would greet the light.

"Thus space for many million will I give," brags Faust, but Mephistopheles is digging him a grave instead of a ditch, and has the last word:

> But all your work is done for us.
> Your dams and dikes will do no good
> For you are cooking Neptune's food:
> That Devil of the Seas will dine quite well.
> In every way you're doomed to fail.
> With the elements we've sworn to prevail,
> And wash it all away to hell.

# Special Places

THERE is an odd similarity between certain wild places and works of art. For those who seek it, of course, there can be beauty in any wild place. Yet there are places where the beauty is so compelling as to seem almost planned, places that seem to reach out and capture the passerby's attention as a painting does.

One approaches such places rather as a bee approaches a flower. Both seem arranged so as to lead the visitor along an attractive structure toward a central experience. The analogy breaks down here because we know that a flower's structure leads a bee toward having pollen adhere to its body, and we don't know of any such reason why beautiful places attract humans. Still, the attraction is a strong and venerable one, as evidenced by our ancient propensity for building temples and shrines in such places. As cultures have become more elaborate, the temples and shrines have tended to obscure the places, but the attraction remains.

When one enters such a place unexpectedly, it can be like opening a nondescript door in a blank wall and stepping suddenly into a cathedral. A few years ago, I stumbled on one beneath Anthony Peak in Mendocino National Forest. The entrance certainly was nondescript: a dusty culvert where the Mendocino Pass road cut across a steep creekbed. The usual star thistles and mulleins grew on the shoulder; the usual jumble of dried mud and dead trees had slid down from the eroding cut; and the usual beverage cans twinkled in the weeds. It could have been anywhere in "the land of many uses."

For some forgotten reason, however, I pulled my car off the road at this unpromising location and, after a couple of false starts, negotiated a way over the steep cut into the woods above. I scrambled through a chaos of manzanita and ceanothus brush and tree saplings, which I'd expected, and abruptly found myself under some of the biggest Douglas firs and canyon live oaks I'd ever seen, which I certainly hadn't expected. From the road, the woods above the cut hadn't appeared different from the second-growth forest of the vicinity, a forest that has been cut repeatedly in the past forty years. But the moss was deep under these trees. This was a shred of virgin forest growing alongside the busiest road within a hundred miles.

I climbed on, half expecting to come to a skid road or an expanse of stumps, but I didn't. I passed through a succession of glades caused by slumping of the steep, unstable slope. Some were sunny, some shady; some were full of tree seedlings, some almost bare of plants. All acquired a certain elegance from the giant trees that stood on the more stable patches of soil around them. Nature may be destructive with its tectonic upheavals, its earthquakes and erosion, but trees take it in stride, which isn't surprising since they've been doing so for several hundred million years.

I could hear the creek through the trees. It was loud, since this was March and snow was melting higher up. I moved in its direction, and came to a cliff overlooking the deep-cut bed. Ancient alders grew along the stream, and their smooth gray trunks, bare of branches for most of their height, reached far above the clifftop, mingling their catkins and swelling leaf buds with the evergreen fir and oak leaves of the forest overstory. The creek was completely canopied by trees, a green cave, but it wasn't gloomy. Enough direct sunlight penetrated to spangle the hazel and ferns on the ground, and the water sparkled on the deep green schist of the creekbed. A fresh breeze carried smells of melting snow from above, and of flowering vegetation from the warm woods along the Black Butte River three thousand feet below. Incense cedars grew along the creek too, and their cinnamon-colored trunks and bright green foliage warmed up the color scheme.

I kept climbing. The creek branched, and one branch was so steep I'd have had to follow it on hands and knees. I followed the other, which grew steeper, then leveled out in a swampy little glen of grass and squawbush and young alders, then steepened again as ponderosa pine and white fir began to replace the Douglas fir and canyon live oak. Patches of snow appeared, and conspired with fallen trunks to make the slope even more taxing, but I kept on. Somehow, I felt there was more at the top of this ravine than a ridgeline or brushfield or talus pile. I don't know why I felt this: perhaps simply because the climb had been surprisingly beautiful so far, or because the slopes of Anthony Peak weren't visible ahead, giving me the impression that some kind of plateau intervened between me and the mountain. Perhaps some "genius loci" was ineffably calling me. In any case, my movement up the creek seemed as directed as a bee's climb into a monkey flower.

The creek forked again, and I again followed the gentler fork, which again grew steeper. The water narrowed to a rivulet in a bed full of pine needles. The ponderosas and white firs grew more thickly than the live oaks and Douglas firs, and weren't as large. Patches of dying manzanita here and there under them indicated that the area had been burned over more than the woods lower down. Large lightning fires would have been a regular occurrence at this elevation before the Forest Service started suppressing them.

Just as the slopes above the creek became so steep and snowy that I had to start walking in the bed, I saw a dimunition of the forest shade ahead. The ravine slopes opened onto a level expanse, and through the trees that covered it, I glimpsed some kind of sunny space. I moved toward it with the excitement hominids seem instinctively to feel on finding an open place in a forest, and stepped suddenly into what might have been a Zen garden.

I had more or less expected to come upon one of the little meadows of tarweeds and bunch grasses that dot Mendocino National Forest. Instead, I found a rocky basin surrounded with boulders and bare gravel. In the center of the basin was a large pool, and in the pool was a boulder so gracefully set off-center that I easily could imagine a crowd of monks carefully placing it there. Around the pool grew elegant clumps of small, gnarled deciduous oaks that might have been bonsais, although I knew they were simply a dwarf variety of the big Garry oaks at lower altitudes. The pool was high with snowmelt and had inundated some of the trees: otherwise the place was so tidy and orderly as to seem tended. But there was no sign of people, only some bear scats left over from the previous autumn, when the acorns had been ripe. On my return, I surprised a small bear that had been sleeping on a bed of shredded bark beside the creek.

I was in a small town in Japan once, and happened on a local shrine, which was on a slope right across the road from the blue-tiled houses with their TV aerials and Hondas. I climbed up an avenue of giant old trees, past a sunken meadow, and then up a shady trail to a glade that contained a strange little cedar box of a building. I know little about Japanese religion, but I could feel that this was a special place. It didn't look like the rocky basin in Mendocino National Forest, but I had a similar experience of both places: first the exhilaration of moving upward through the ancient trees, and the awe of stepping into an open—but enclosed and secret—place that was imbued with a sense of creative presence. Someone once told me that the spirits of such places take the form of small animals. Sure enough, a tiny brown frog was sitting before the little old shrine in Japan, and its trans-Pacific counterparts were singing lustily around the basin in California. A troop of western gray squirrels, usually a very timid species, followed me through the little oaks as though watchful of my good behavior.

The difference between the American place and the Japanese one is that the Japanese has been recognized and revered by the dominant culture for centuries, whereas the American has no official recognition, except to the extent that it is included in a public natural resource and recreation area. Americans are lucky to still have so much land that such places can be virtually unknown. Yet I think this points up a dangerous gap in our relationship with wild places.

Americans have an enthusiasm for big spectacular places and for smaller ones if they are scientifically or recreationally significant. For the little, special places that dot every natural landscape, however, we have a certain cultural blindness. We live largely in cities, and when we leave them, we don't have much time to wander at random. We throng the established parks and wilderness areas, and we stay on the trails, hurrying past many a special place on the way to the next lake or designated campsite.

If the places we hurry past are within established parks and wilderness areas, it's perhaps just as well that we ignore them. There have to be places where small bears can nap in peace. Unfortunately, most special places aren't inside parks and wilderness areas, and our official conservation bodies have no mandate or mechanism that I know of for protecting them. If a rare plant or animal lives in one, the Interior Department or Forest Service might be persuaded (if enough public pressure mounts) to offer it some administrative protection. But if a rare beauty or spirit lives there? When Robinson Jeffers wrote of "beautiful places killed like rabbits," he was being exact. With our chain saws and tractors, we extinguish beauty even more efficiently than we do rare organisms.

The big trees and rocky basin under Anthony Peak are many miles from the nearest wilderness area, the Yolla Bolly–Middle Eel. The Forest Service has designated a natural area on the peak, but it also has spoken of establishing a downhill ski area on it. Anyway, the trees and basin are a long way below the peak. Logging has intensified in the forest under the Reagan administration. It seems as though a truck is coming down Mendocino Pass road every ten minutes as I write this. When I see the stack of pine and fir logs on the back of one, I wonder if they come from a place that was special once, but that isn't any more.

# At the End of the Earth

ONE day in June 1972, I decided to go to Alaska. The next morning I threw some things in a backpack, walked down to U.S. 101, and stuck out my thumb. Two weeks later I stood at a crossing somewhere between Juneau and Fairbanks. It had been an interesting trip, but not an easy one. I had met surprisingly friendly and accommodating people, but there had been much standing by the road, dodging rocks thrown by the passing trucks (a major hazard on the "gravel" Alaska Highway), and many encounters with a frontier mentality that dismissed wildlife, Indians, and environmentalists as worthless obstructions.

In a way it was a crossroads in my life: between dreams of a cabin in the wilderness and less romantic considerations, one of which was a suspicion that the cabin-builder, whatever his intentions, is as much a spreader of civilization and its discontents as an escapee from them. It was not too hard a choice. I am not the pioneer type. I backpacked a little in the St. Elias Mountains ("Watch out for the grizzly," a local man told me, "he chased a jeep last week."), then caught the ferry for Juneau and points south. "The Great land" seemed a little *too* great.

My impulsive, ambivalent jaunt was a bit like the American experience in Alaska as a whole. We acquired it on impulse, and we have been ambivalent about it ever since, torn between dark visions of howling polar wastes and bright ones of golden arctic empires. One might say that Alaska is a crossroads for America, a crossroads between dreams of an infinitely accommodating planet where any number of people can find their cabin in the wilderness and less romantic considerations.

Secretary of State William Seward would not have liked hearing his 1867 purchase of Russia's North American possession called "impulsive," but at the time it was called much worse. The possibility remains that Alaska could have become part of Canada if Britain had been friendlier to the United States government during the Civil War. Alaska was a logical extension of British dominion: The Hudson's Bay Company already had wrested fur concessions there from the czar, who was more interested in Siberia. But Russia did not want the British Empire as an eastern neighbor, so it agreed to sell us Alaska for $7 million. Seward convinced a highly ambivalent Congress to close the deal on the grounds that Russia had been friendly to the United States during the war and deserved a pat on the back.

We had only the vaguest idea of what we were getting, further evidence of impulsiveness. Alaska remained mysterious long after its European discovery in 1741 by Vitus Bering (who never even stepped onto the mainland). The Bering Expedition was haunted by mists, storms, disease, and still-unexplained disappearances. The only real objective proof it produced by reaching North America was a blue-crested jay shot by expedition naturalist Georg Wilhelm Steller on Kayak Island. Steller recognized a relationship between the new species (which has been named after him) and the eastern blue jay, a picture of which he had seen in an American natural history book.

Russia's only real interest in Alaska was the fur trade, so it confined its explorations to the coast, where sea otters and fur seals were mainstays of the trade, and to occasional forays up the rivers to buy marten, fox, and other inland pelts from the natives. In 1867 Alaska was unsurveyed, its boundaries with Canada unclear, its interior a blank. Mount McKinley and the other peaks of the central Alaska Range would not be described by white men until 1896, the Canadian boundary would not be established until the turn of the century, and the far northern Brooks Range would go unexplored until Robert Marshall's expeditions of the 1920s and 1930s. As far as Western (or Eastern) civilization was concerned, Alaska was the end of the earth.

When superimposed over a map of the lower forty-eight states, Alaska's 589,800 square miles stretch from Georgia to Minnesota to California and blot out most of the Midwest, so there was much to explore. The congressmen who derided "Seward's folly" as an undifferentiated frozen waste—an "Icebergia" or "Walrussia"—could be excused. Of course, they were wrong. Alaska is anything but undifferentiated. The iceberg part is different from the frozen part, and the walrus frequents neither. Much of Alaska is no colder than New England. The southern part (including the southeastern panhandle, the Alaska and Kenai peninsulas, and the Aleutian Islands) is bathed by the warm, moist air of the Japanese Current, so it receives up to 220 inches of rain a year and has relatively mild winters. Because of the rain, southeast Alaska has some of the densest forests and, around its mountaintops, the biggest iceberg-calving glaciers on the continent.

Glaciers are, of course, ice. Still the *real* frozen part of Alaska lies inland from the southern coast. Cut off from the Japanese Current, the interior mountains and valleys of the Yukon, Kuskokwim, and other rivers have only light rainfall and some of the coldest winter temperatures on earth, down to minus seventy-five degrees Fahrenheit at Fort Yukon. Most soil is permanently frozen a foot or so beneath the surface, and a good thing, too, because the area would be semidesert if the permafrost did not hold the meager rain near the surface, making it available to poplar and willow, and thus to moose and snowshoe hare. Even so, the contrast between coastal forest and interior bush is a little like that between California and Nevada.

Beyond the Brooks Range, the North Slope actually is warmer than the interior valleys because it borders on the Arctic Ocean. It also is even drier than the interior because the icy Arctic Ocean produces little atmospheric moisture. With yearly rainfall as low as four inches at Point Barrow, the North Slope would be a real desert if its soil was not frozen. Instead, it is mostly tundra, a spongy mat of lichen, moss, and stunted angiosperms that offers a surprising quantity of food to animals (especially nesting birds) in the uninterrupted light of arctic summer, but in winter is so inhospitable that even the lichen-eating caribou leave it for the interior spruce forest. The walrus, the polar bear, and the white whale, so dear to the hearts of Seward's sardonic congressional opponents, mostly are confined to this arctic coast and to the west coast bordering the Bering Sea, where conditions are similar because the Aleutian Islands cut off the Japanese Current.

Yet Alaska is not a wasteland all year round. Nothing surprised me more than the density and boldness of the wildlife. I had expected it to be spectacular, but sparse and elusive. On my hike into the St. Elias Mountains, I saw a lynx, several moose, and more signs of black and grizzly bear than I was altogether prepared for. In southeast Alaska, mink, bald eagles, and humpback whales seemed as ubiquitous as cats, pigeons, and cows in the lower forty-eight. Of course, I was in one of the richer parts of the state in summer: one can walk for days on winter tundra and see no life. Under pressure from climate, Alaskan wildlife is less diverse than that of temperate or tropical zones and thus less stable and more prone to boom and bust cycles. I saw a lynx because it was a good year for snowshoe hares, on which lynx mostly prey: in another year I might have seen neither. Still, Alaska's wildlife supported the estimated 74,000 people who lived there when Bering arrived. It seems a tiny population today, but it probably was proportional to Europe's Paleolithic population.

The fur and fishing industries never doubted Alaska's value. American ownership brought rapid and efficient exploitation of both resources, perpetuating a boom and bust pattern for Alaskan development as seemingly endless abundance sooner or later proved otherwise. The Russians almost had exterminated the fur seals by 1835, but had adopted conservation measures and built up the Pribilof herd to 3 million seals by 1867. American conservation measures proved ineffective against uncontrolled pelagic sealing, and the herd dwindled to 100,000 by 1911. Sea otters were reduced to an estimated 500 during that same period. Whales and walrus became so scarce that charitable settlers imported reindeer from Siberia in the 1880s for the

Eskimo to live on. Alaska's abundant Pacific salmon runs lasted longer, but scores of canneries operating hundreds of fish traps that automatically scooped up the runs as they entered the rivers eventually depressed production from a peak of over 700 million pounds a year in the late thirties to less than 300 million in the early fifties.

Such an assault on the native fauna was the normal first stage of any American frontier. In Alaska, however, it was not followed by a wave of settlement, as in the lower forty-eight. This is not to say that thousands of Americans did not head for Sitka, the first capital, and points north after 1867, but most turned back disappointed. Alaska's population remained stable or even declined as other frontiers filled up. The reasons for this have long been a subject of argument. Development boosters such as former governor Ernest Gruening (in his 1954 book, *The State of Alaska*) have blamed it on an unholy alliance of government bureaucracy, which would not survey or patent land claims, and on absentee fur and fishing companies, which suppressed competition from local entrepreneurs. There is some truth to this, particularly as regards a salmon industry that preferred migrant to local labor, but the sheer ruggedness of the land probably had more to do with Alaska's slow growth. American settlers were mostly farmers, and Alaska defied traditional agriculture.

Alaska's development largely has been of the sporadic, industrial sort, what Wendell Berry aptly has called "unsettling." Along with fur and fishing came mining: hopeful prospectors from California and Nevada were among the first American immigrants in 1867. Gold brought settlement to Juneau in the 1880s, and discoveries in Canada's neighboring Yukon Territory brought as many as 80,000 goldseekers to southeast Alaska in the great rushes of 1897 and 1898. These miners spilled out into the interior drainage of the Yukon River and to Nome at the tip of the Seward Peninsula in the early twentieth century. Beginning with primitive nineteenth-century sourdough methods, the gold industry graduated to massive hydraulic mining development during the first three decades of the twentieth century, washing away entire riverbanks with high-powered hoses (and incidentally exhuming prehistoric animals entombed in the permafrost). Deposits of tin, copper, and other metals were sought in amazingly remote places. Then came fossil fuels. In 1914 the Wilson administration began the Alaska Railroad as a way of making Alaskan coal available to the Pacific Fleet. In 1924, as the fleet was converting to oil, the Harding administration set aside the Indiana-sized Naval Petroleum Reserve Four on the North Slope. Alaska began to look more and more valuable.

Yet there still were powerful forces working against headlong industrialization. Again, the land's ruggedness probably was the main obstacle. Without a road linking it to the lower forty-eight states, with few enough roads of any sort, Alaska beckoned to the lustful entrepreneur from behind a wall of muskeg. And the federal government *was* more restrictive than during the settlement of the lower forty-eight, not simply from meanness, as Ernest Gruening seemed to think, but because the ill effects of its laissez-faire attitude toward earlier speculators were becoming too evident. Theodore Roosevelt did not establish the Tongass and Chugach national forests to impoverish Alaskans, but to ensure that the rapacious practices of the Maine and Minnesota timber barons would not be repeated in southeast Alaska. Although Alaskans burned Gifford Pinchot in effigy, the first chief of the Forest Service had no desire to lock up their forests: he simply wanted them cut scientifically and economically.

Of course, the federal government did not act to conserve Sitka spruce and fur seals from simple altruism any more than from simple meanness. It was a different government from its Gilded Age antecedents. It had twentieth-century responsibilities—fleets, expeditionary forces, an overseas empire. It no longer could afford simply to hand out resources freely: it needed a percentage. Such needs increased as the 1930s depression placed new social responsibilities upon it. The New Deal was interested in Alaskan development as a possible remedy for poverty in the lower forty-eight states: it sent hand-picked settlers north in special convoys. Then the Japanese and Soviet threats brought unprecedented federal development as the

AlCan Highway and many other military roads opened up formerly inaccessible areas to business and settlement.

World War II saw private industry adapting to the ways of big government. The salmon and fur industries always had kept powerful lobbies with the federal bureaus that regulated them. Now timber and oil flexed their Alaskan muscles with Agriculture and Interior. Clear-cut areas and a pulp industry appeared in the Tongass. Oil moved into the Kenai Moose Range (which President Franklin Delano Roosevelt had set aside from the Chugach National Forest by executive order) after a big strike in the late fifties and began stepping up explorations elsewhere. After 1959, Alaska's new state government became an advocate of government-industry cooperation in gigantic projects such as the Rampart Dam, wherein the Army Corps of Engineers was to impound the Yukon River for the utilities industry. For Alaska's long-suffering boosters, it must have seemed like a millennium.

Yet the Rampart Dam was not built, and it was not stopped by climate, terrain, or government restrictions. (Not entirely, anyway.) By 1963, when the dam was proposed, another force had begun opposing development as though in reaction to the growing symbiosis between government and industry. It must have come as a surprise to the Ernest Gruenings, who had spent careers trying to wrest Alaska's riches from lower forty-eight control, to find their plans being questioned and opposed for the sake of brown bears and old-growth trees (which Gruening invariably called "over-ripe and dying on the stump"). It must have seemed a little like a stab in the back, because Alaska's scenery and wildlife always had been big drawing cards for the boosters. They attracted new residents and tourism, potentially a major industry. But this new force was saying some economic development would have to be deferred or foregone to protect the scenery and wildlife.

What we today call the conservation or environmental movement has been in Alaska almost as long as government and industry, but it took much longer to get organized. One might say that it first manifested itself when the Pribilof Islands fur seal reserve was established in 1869, but this would be stretching it, since the reserve was more for the benefit of sealers than seals and was ineffective anyway. The movement certainly had arrived when John Muir explored Glacier Bay in 1879 and when Muir and John Burroughs participated in the Harriman Alaskan Expedition in 1899. President Theodore Roosevelt established the first Alaskan migratory bird refuges along the coast in 1909, and President William Howard Taft added to them in 1912.

A distinguished roster of explorers, naturalists, and scientists successively fought for protection of various choice bits of Alaska. Big-game hunter Charles Sheldon successfully lobbied for creation of Alaska's first national park to protect the exceptional concentration of game he had discovered north of Mount McKinley. Geologist Robert Griggs explored and campaigned for preservation of the dramatic volcanic region that became Katmai National Monument in 1918. Botanist William S. Cooper urged Calvin Coolidge to establish a national monument for the receding glaciers and advancing forests of Glacier Bay. Writer-photographer John Holzworth drew attention to the brown bears and bald eagles of Admiralty Island.

Alaska was not simply a cause for wilderness protectors: it was a breeding ground of them. The Forest Service's Robert Marshall gave the name "Gates of the Arctic" to a mountain pass in the Brooks Range during his personal expeditions and was a cofounder of the Wilderness Society. Olaus Murie, director of the Wilderness Society for seventeen years, spent years exploring and studying wildlife in the Aleutians and Interior Alaska and was instrumental in getting the 9-million-acre Arctic National Wildlife Refuge established in 1960. The National Park Service continued Marshall's exploratory work in the 1950s and 1960s and identified thirty-nine potential additions to the National Park System. Grassroots Alaskan groups appeared, such as the Alaska Conservation Society, organized in 1960 to fight Project Chariot, an Atomic Energy Commission plan to open a harbor in northwestern Alaska with a nuclear blast.

Conservation accomplishments were significant, but they were piecemeal, with different groups working separately, always a problem in trying to protect a planet wherein everything is connected to everything else. In the late sixties, however, events began to occur that would bring conservationists together in an unprecedented and highly effective way. Alaska statehood had touched off a number of land conflicts as the state began to select the lands it would be granted. Not least of these were the aboriginal claims of the Alaska natives. In 1966 and 1969, Interior Secretary Stewart Udall put a freeze on much of the public domain in Alaska, prohibiting transfer to state or other hands until native claims were settled. These "twice-frozen" lands included most of the areas identified by the Park Service as worthy of protection.

The Prudhoe Bay oil strike of 1968 evoked a great eagerness on the part of the development-minded to get the native claims settled so that the oil industry could build an 800-mile pipeline from the North Slope to the southern port of Valdez. Conservationists had big oil over a barrel. After unsuccessful attempts to get Lyndon Johnson to establish national monuments and other unsuccessful attempts to stop the pipeline, they settled down for the long haul. The Alaska Native Claims Settlement Act of 1971 provided for native lands and set the stage for the pipeline: it contained sections 17(d)(1) and 17(d)(2), which, in effect, made the government withdraw at least 80 millions acres of prime Alaskan scenery and wildlife habitat for consideration as parks, refuges, and other reserves; it also required the government to act on these withdrawals within seven years.

Interior Secretary Rogers C. B. Morton launched studies of the Alaska lands in 1971, but the proposals he recommended in 1973 disappointed conservationists. With legislation in abeyance, they used the next few years building a national activist network around the Alaska Coalition, which had been established to fight the pipeline, a group that eventually would include fifty-three organizations—labor and business groups as well as conservationists. When the more conservation-minded Carter administration took office in January 1977, the coalition was ready to move, and a good thing too, since the Native Claims Act's deadline was less than two years away.

Congressman Udall immediately introduced H.R. 39, which proposed to set aside almost 115 million acres of Alaska for ecological purposes. House Interior subcommittee hearings, chaired by Congressman John Seiberling (D-Ohio), produced an unprecedented outpouring of pro-wilderness sentiment during that spring and summer. Under the leadership of Udall and Seiberling, the bill reached the House floor in April 1978 and passed by an extraordinary 277–31 vote despite opposition from Alaska Representative Don Young, the state of Alaska, and industry.

The fight had just begun, however. Alaska Senators Mike Gravel(D) and Ted Stevens(R) opposed the Senate counterpart of H.R. 39. With Gravel threatening to block it completely and Stevens working to weaken it in committee, the bill did not reach the Senate floor. Under attack by well-funded lobbies for the oil and timber industry, the National Rifle Association, and the Alaska state government, the bill had been so weakened as to be unacceptable to both conservationists and the administration. It protected one-third less land than the 124.6 million acres that H.R. 39 would have added to four national conservation systems (national park, national forest, national wildlife refuge, and wild and scenic rivers) and only half as much wilderness as the 65.5 million acres listed in H.R. 39.

Attempts at a compromise between the various factions failed when Gravel suddenly demanded a half-dozen commercial access corridors through key conservation units, and the 95th Congress ended without a Senate vote on the legislation. Senator Gravel also stymied a measure to extend the 1971 Native Claims Act's December 1978 deadline, and it was fast approaching.

The Carter administration came to the rescue in the most daring executive action for conservation since Theodore Roosevelt withdrew the national forests. On 1 December, under provisions of the 1906 Antiquities Act, the president signed an executive order creating 56 million acres of Alaskan national monuments, including most of the lands Congress had designated for national parks. Under the Federal Land Policy and Management Act of 1976, he also directed Interior Secretary Cecil Andrus to establish 40 million acres of wildlife refuges in Alaska and directed Agriculture Secretary Bob Bergland to withdraw 11 million acres in the Tongass and Chugach national forests. Carter's actions protected most of the lands H.R. 39 would have, in effect giving Congress more time to pass legislation.

Industry lobbyists watered down H.R. 39 as it passed through committee in 1979, but Udall and Representative John Anderson (R-Illinois) introduced a substitute bill that passed the House 268–157 in May 1979 with the help of intensive Alaska Coalition lobbying. Again, however, the Alaska delegation delayed and weakened the Senate bill, and although Senator Paul Tsongas (D-Massachusetts) introduced a better substitute, Alaska lands legislation failed to reach the Senate floor in 1979 and early 1980. The first test vote on the Senate floor in July 1980 proved unexpectedly favorable to conservationists, however, and Senator Gravel's delaying tactics had begun to irritate his colleagues. After behind-the-scenes negotiations, a compromise bill passed the Senate 78–14 on 19 August.

The Senate bill set aside over 104 million acres, 97 million of them in the national park and wildlife refuge systems. It was less land than the House or the administration had set aside, and the protection it afforded that land was less complete. Many southeastern Alaska national forest wilderness areas were left out of the Senate bill, including nearly 150,000 acres of Misty Fjords National Monument where U.S. Borax wanted to mine molybdenum. Federal funding was provided to support logging in Southeast Alaska's Tongass National Forest. The Senate bill placed parts of the Yukon Flats under the multiple-use Bureau of Land Management instead of under the Fish and Wildlife Service as the House bill had done. It eliminated two important wildlife refuges—the Copper River Delta in the Southeast and the Teshekpuk-Utukok on the North Slope. It mandated oil and gas exploration in the Arctic National Wildlife Refuge and a transportation corridor through the wilderness of Gates of the Arctic National Park and Preserve, as well as reducing the protected corridors along wild and scenic rivers.

Conservationists girded to win back some of the losses in House-Senate conference, but history intervened. The election of an outspoken, anti-environmentalist administration under Ronald Reagan ended hope that the legislation could be improved in the near future, and Udall reluctantly urged the House to accept the Senate bill. President Carter signed the Alaska National Interest Lands Conservation Act (ANILCA) on 2 December 1980, in a ceremony attended by legislators, Alaska natives, conservationists, citizen activists, and industry lobbyists. Sierra Club Alaska Task Force Chairman Edgar Wayburn summed up the mood of many when he told newsmen: "The act is not an end, but a beginning."

ANILCA was flawed when enacted, and its administration under President Reagan has been even more imperfect. Still, it looms Denali-like over the scattered islands of ecological integrity in the lower forty-eight. The act more than doubled the national park system and tripled the national wildlife refuge and wilderness systems. Additionally, it set out to do what has never been done before: to *integrally* protect the wilderness of what amounts to a subcontinent; not simply to save bits and pieces as they are threatened or as they happen to become available for protection, but to tie it together, the frozen part and the iceberg part and the walrus part; to maintain an articulated organism of wilderness around the busy body of Alaskan civilization.

Comprehending it all is too much for one person. I suspect it is too much for one generation, for a score of generations. The real significance of what has been done, and must continue to be done, may not emerge for thousands, or even millions, of years. We are not just protecting walrus and polar bear and caribou, we are protecting a world, pretty much the same world that some of our reindeer-hunting ancestors inhabited 50,000 years ago, a world that evolved as the Pleistocene ice sheet plowed across the continents, driving the older world of warm grassland and broadleaf forest southward. It is a vulnerable but strong and sustaining world, a world that some remote descendants of ours may needing someday, when the ice sheets return. North America will be a lonely place then, if the walrus and caribou and polar bear are gone.

# IV  WILDLIFE

# The Importance of Predators

**W**HEN Cotton Mather said that "what is not useful is vicious," he made a definitive statement of one American attitude toward nature. It is a philosophical attitude as well as an economic one. For Mather and his fellow Puritans, wild nature was fallen, an abode of Satan. It could only be redeemed by domesticating it, by making it over into an approximation of the Garden of Eden, where man would rule harmoniously over peaceful and subservient animals, where, as Isaiah had prophesied, the lion would lie down with the lamb.

The Puritans found a distinctly unsubservient lion when they arrived in Massachusetts. (They thought the native puma was the same as the African lion until its lack of a mane eventually convinced them otherwise.) And the lion was only one species. The New England wilderness supported a diversity and abundance of predators, in numbers and kinds that seem a little fantastic to us today. Imagine, for example, a Massachusetts where a one-penny bounty was paid on timber wolves, as was the case in 1630, or where serious consideration was given to *fencing* Cape Cod to keep wolves out, as in 1717. One seventeenth-century author went so far as to say that wolves were "the greatest inconvenience the Countrey hath, both for matter of dammage to private men in particular, and the whole Countrey in general." Nothing was more opposite to the Puritan ideal of redemption through domestication than the predator. Not only was it a threat to livestock, but its very way of life—noisily or silently pursuing prey, untidily dismembering and devouring it—was a challenge to the entire spectrum of Puritan values: decorum, neatness, frankness, gravity. The predator was a kind of compendium of all that was undesirable in man as well as nature. Yet for us there are moral ambiguities in the Puritans' view. If the wolves who killed and ate sheep and deer were evil, what did that make the men who killed and ate sheep and deer? If killing was evil, what did that make the men who killed wolves? The Puritans' view of man and nature did not admit to such ambiguities, but in a world of dwindling wolves and growing violence and cruelty, we increasingly are troubled by them. We suspect that we have not understood the predator and the living world of which it is a part.

The Puritan attitude toward predators has been the prevalent one during most of America's history, and the rise of the United States saw a sharp decline of native carnivores. Still common in Massachusetts in 1700, wolves were extinct there a century later and disappeared from New England by the mid-nineteenth century. The wolves of the South and West didn't last much longer, though costly government extermination campaigns were required to remove the big, wide-ranging buffalo wolves from the High Plains. Mountain lions, grizzly bears, and other large predators succumbed to less systematic persecution in most of the country at roughly the same time as wolves. Smaller species such as the marten, otter, mink, and bobcat also declined or disappeared in many areas, either through direct persecution or as a result of the poisoning and trapping of wolves.

Until the 1930s, predators were not even welcome in national parks, wildlife refuges, or other nature preserves, which were conceived as retreats for "useful" animals such as ducks, deer, or songbirds. Government hunters killed so many mountain lions in Yellowstone Park that the species has never recovered there, and Yosemite proved no refuge for the California grizzly bear, even though the park was established in 1867, about sixty years before the grizzly's extermination in that state. Predator control in parks and refuges was justified in some cases because populations of prey animals had been so decimated by overhunting by humans. But in most cases, as with the Yellowstone lions and Yosemite grizzlies, predator control simply was a general policy premised on the idea that predators were useless and vicious, an idea that many early twentieth-century scientists and conservationists, notably Theodore Roosevelt and William Hornaday (a founder of the Bronx Zoo and the National Wildlife Federation), found acceptable. (Roosevelt did urge the government not to kill *too* many lions in Glacier National Park, thus perhaps saving that population.)

There is another American attitude toward predators, historically less prevalent than the Puritans' but probably just as old, although its early expression was so sporadic that its origin is difficult to place. It is exemplified in the writings of William Bartram, a Colonial naturalist and artist, who explored the Carolinas, Georgia, and Florida in the 1770s. Bartram spent years camping near wolves, bears, lions, and alligators (18 feet was not an unusual length for alligators then), and never showed any particular dislike for them except on the rare occasions when they directly threatened him. He did, however, express considerable regret at witnessing the wanton killing of a bear cub and a wolf pup, and once he appeared thankful for the apparent forbearance of a wolf that had robbed him of some fish while he was asleep: "How much easier and more eligible might it have been for him to have leaped upon my breast in the dead of night and torn my throat . . . than to have made protracted and circular approaches, and then after, by chance, espying the fish over my head, with the greatest caution and silence to rear up and take them off the snags one by one . . .?"

Bartram was a farmer, like most people in the American colonies, but he was also two other things that set him apart from the Puritans. First, he was a Quaker and thus inclined to take a less militant approach to the redemption of the American wilds. Second, he was an enthusiastic woodsman and hunter, and thus prone to certain ideas that the Puritans did not entertain. (Puritans viewed hunting and woodcraft much as they viewed taverns and dancing.) An imaginative hunter such as Bartram was likely to discern a certain similarity between the wolf, the lion, and himself. Because hunting was useful and good for him, it might be so for wolves and lions. Indeed, it might be so in some general way that links the lives of domesticated men and wild animals.

It is difficult to point to a seminal literary source for Bartram's tolerant attitude toward predators in the same way that one can point to the Bible for the Puritans' attitude. (The Bible was written by goat- and sheepherding people who lived in a land of leopards and wolves as well as milk and honey. Like many Middle Eastern and African pastoralists, the biblical tribes seem to have been neither enthusiastic nor adept as hunters.) Perhaps Bartram's attitude is simply a residue of the hunting-and-gathering way of life from which all human cultures have emerged in the past 15,000 years—a residue that was overshadowed by the new agricultural life, but never fully obliterated. As hunting was handed down as a sideline or sport, a set of attitudes went with it that often were at odds with agricultural ones. Bartram probably learned something of his attitude toward predators from the Creek Indians, who combined farming and hunting in an apparently harmonious way, allowing packs of red wolves (*Canis niger,* now an endangered species) to live right alongside their horse and cattle herds.

Bartram also was influenced by the so-called natural philosophers, who had been increasing in numbers and influence since the Renaissance. They saw nature not as an abode of evil but as a smoothly functioning mechanism created by a rational, beneficent deity. If predators were part of such a world, reasoned the philosophers, there must be a good reason for them. John Bruckner, a French author, proposed one in 1768 in his *Philosophical Survey of the Animal Creation*: "The effects of the carnivorous race are exactly the same as that of the pruning hook, with respect to shrubs which are too luxuriant in their growth, or of the hoe to plants that grow too close together. By the diminution of their number, the others grow to perfection."

Equating predators with hoes and pruning hooks would have outraged the Puritans, and seems overly anthropomorphic today, but Bruckner's statement is significant because it contains the germs of evolution and ecology, the scientific disciplines by which the modern world understands nature. The idea of the predator as a check on the "too luxuriant" numbers of its prey is an ecological idea, and the idea of the prey "growing to perfection" by the predator's "pruning" is an evolutionary one. Both ideas have been central to the development of biological science. Far from seeing predation as a flaw in, and threat to, the living world, Bruckner's scientific descendants have seen it as one of the creative foundations of life, a maintainer of ecological stability and promoter of beneficial natural selection.

It's not difficult to see why this benign view of predators took much longer to catch on than the Puritans' intolerant one. It's one thing for a leisured gentleman (as many early scientists were) to discern the benefits of predation on fossil horses or African zebras, quite another for a farmer to discern them in a wolf's killing of weak or sickly livestock. But the benign view did assert itself, as ideas often do, just when its opponent seemed to have won—when the Puritan ethic had killed off the big predators and was going to work on the small ones.

Quite suddenly, in the 1920s, the wolves and lions did not seem so threatening any more, or the deer and sheep so harmless. In Pennsylvania and the upper Midwest, where the last wolves and lions had been killed one or two decades before, exploding deer herds ate the woods bare and attacked crops, then starved to death in winter snow. On western range, semi-desert conditions were spreading as sagebrush and mesquite replaced grassland eaten bare by sheep. The classic display of "too luxuriant" deer and livestock was Arizona's Kaibab Plateau, from which more than 6,000 wolves, lions, coyotes, and bobcats (as well as golden eagles and other raptors) were eliminated by government hunters in the first two decades of this century. Under pressure from livestock and from a deer herd that had increased from 4,000 to 100,000, "the whole country looked as though a swarm of locusts had swept through it . . . torn, gray, stripped, and dying." Government scientists such as the Forest Service's Aldo Leopold, who had promoted predator control in the Southwest while happily blasting any wolf that strayed into his sights, began to have second thoughts. The Puritan view of nature seemed turned upside-down. It no longer was the ravening jaws of the wolf that threatened the stability and safety of the world but the jaws of the lamb and the fawn. In its sudden absence, the predator began to seem a lost element of balance.

Such thoughts were not shared by the United States Congress, which in 1931 passed the "Eradication and Control of Predatory and Other Wild Animals Act" under which our present system of federal predator control is administered. With traps and cyanide before World War II, and with Compound 1080 afterward, a vigorous campaign has been waged against predators. Its tacit goal, if one listened to livestock-industry spokesmen, was eradication from virtually all grazing lands outside national parks of any wild animal that might threaten a lamb. The campaign had almost succeeded in eradicating at least two species, the black-footed ferret and red wolf, when it ran afoul of the burgeoning environmental movement in the late 1960s. Two presidential commissions and one executive order later, the use of 1080 was largely discontinued, and the idea that predators that *weren't* killing livestock might be tolerated outside parks gained some official standing.

America is currently in a cold war with predators. Although the nation is no longer officially committed to their total destruction, predators must still contend with federal trapping and poison programs, with a fur industry that has killed more coyotes and bobcats in recent years than have predator-control programs themselves, and with the pollution and habitat destruction from which all wildlife suffers. The big predators of the lower forty-eight states, the wolf, grizzly, and lion, enjoy some official protection in areas where they've gotten rare enough to seem threatened. Whether that protection will suffice in the face of the unofficial persecution they still undergo in an open question. The West is still wild as far as predators go: many ranchers shoot first and ask questions later. The livestock industry recently has succeeded in forcing the Environmental Protection Agency to permit a return to the use of Compound 1080, citing a population explosion of coyotes (in fact, federal studies do not show a substantial increase in numbers of coyotes).

Meanwhile, the question of predators' usefulness or lack thereof has acquired some recent complications that seem a little ironic. One the one hand, scientific studies have cast some doubt on the ecological importance of the predator's "pruning" role. For example, Paul L. Errington's studies of mink and muskrats in Iowa marshes showed that numbers of muskrats are influenced much more by social and environmental factors than by mink predation. Errington found that a nucleus of healthy muskrats with access to food and shelter was virtually immune to mink attack (he even found a fat muskrat and a mink occupying different rooms in the same lodge), and that mink were dependent for prey on surplus muskrats that wandered outside this "zone of safety." In effect, muskrats regulated their own numbers as strong individuals excluded weak ones from food and shelter. One also might say that muskrats controlled *mink* numbers, rather than vice-versa, since mink could not prosper unless enough healthy, safe muskrats were breeding to produce a surplus.

Such studies cast new light on the extreme deer overpopulation near the turn of the century, suggesting that other factors than a lack of predators were at work. Deer found an unprecedentedly large supply of browse in the logged and burned forests of the early twentieth century, and they are more tolerant of crowding than muskrats, so their populations might have exploded even if predators had been present, although the explosions wouldn't have been so disastrous. The most recent theories suggest that predators *can* contribute to a reduction in prey populations, but usually only after a population has begun to decline on its own and many are weak from disease, starvation, or other stress.

The classic enemy of the predator, the American farming population, has undergone a drastic decline of its own in the past half-century, under pressure from an industrial economy that views land not as a potential Eden but as raw material. In a sense, the "usefulness" of the farmer is in doubt. The effects of this on the human-predator relationship are difficult to predict, since nothing like it has happened before. Adaptable predators such as the coyote and raven have benefited from depopulation of marginal farming districts, reoccupying them or, in the coyote's case, moving in for the first time. In prime areas such as the Midwest, however, industrial farming is becoming so efficient that virtually no wildlife is left on which predators can live. Should the industrial economy ever conclude that predators are bad for business, furthermore, its arsenal against them would be infinitely more formidable than the family farmer's. If certain trends continue, both farmer and predator may find themselves "useless" in a landscape of machines and robots that has no similarity to wilderness *or* Eden.

Such a prospect leads one to wonder if the predator-farmer conflict is such a necessary one. If both are threatened by a robot world, they must have something in common. How, after all, did the Puritans prevail in New England? Although they disapproved of hunting, they did not hesitate to practice it. One might say they prevailed by being better predators than the native ones. The conventional notion of the predator as some largish bird or mammal that steals chickens is a biological caricature. Chickens are predators too, as anybody who has seen them go after a snake will agree.

Predation is much more central to life than Cotton Mather, or even John Bruckner, could have imagined. It lies at the root of evolution. Animals very likely never would have evolved beyond a rudimentary, algae-grazing protozoan if some hadn't begun preying on others. They complex food chains that make up modern ecosystems never would have come about. Whether or not plant-eaters *need* to be "pruned" by predators, they *will* be pruned. If we killed every hawk and owl in the world, for example, evolution would start filling their abandoned niches with other species. Birds that now prey on small rodents and songbirds for a part of their diet—jays, crows, ravens, shrikes— would start to do it more. Most predators are, of necessity, quick learners.

Every time we exterminate a predator, we are in a sense creating a new predator. When we exterminated the wolf in New England, we created the New England coyote. We could control the wolf fairly easily because its highly developed social structure put a ceiling on its population growth. It's not so easy to control the coyote, which is more anarchic in its breeding habits. Scientists have estimated that 75 percent of a given coyote population would have to be killed every year for fifty years to exterminate that population. Even then, other coyotes probably would come in from elsewhere. They like to travel.

Predation is a larger phenomenon than our notions of usefulness. At least, it is larger than our *quantitative* notions of usefulness. The biggest, fastest computer won't tell us if predators are costing us more by eating livestock than they are saving us by eating rodents. The dynamics of predation are too complex and variable for the bottom line. As Paul Errington said: "Nature's way is any way that works." Our notion of usefulness usually has been quantitative, concerned with getting enough to live well on. If we value life on this planet, however, and we choose not to turn our eyes away from it—as the Puritans turned their eyes toward the heavens and the industrial economy turns its eyes toward outer space—we need a large notion. It is not only the quantity of things that sustains us here but the *quality* of them.

Indeed, it is the quality that mainly sustains us. We need not simply food but *good* food. When we speak of preserving wildness in the world, we are speaking of preserving quality. Isn't it presumptuous to say that we must preserve wildness in a world that is now, and is likely to remain, largely ice cap, ocean, desert, muskeg, and tropical bush? Wildness has its negative as well as its positive side: a mountain stripped bare by logging, grazing, and erosion is not less wild than it was before its "development," it merely is less good, of lowered quality. Wildness is a fundamental condition of the biosphere, which we can "preserve" only in a qualitative sense. We have no choice about wildness, but we *can* choose between the wildness of the Norway rat and the pariah dog and that of the rabbit and the coyote.

Quality is a standard by which predators have readily discernible uses. They do improve the health and vigor of prey by weeding out sickness and weakness. Perhaps more important from a human viewpoint, they are beautiful, both in themselves and as part of the landscape. An Ohio pasture is more beautiful, more alive and interesting, with a fox on it, as an Alaskan mountain is more so with a wolf on it. Even a garden is more beautiful with a cat in it—an unredeemed predator if there ever was one. I get much more enjoyment from watching coyotes in the hills around this valley than from watching deer. The coyotes simply *do* more. They play with bones, hide them from each other, peer curiously into the river, chase deer for the fun of it. There is something almost deliberately comical about a coyote doodling along through the digger pines and blue oaks with its tongue hanging out and its eyes almost closed. It seems to smile, happy with its raffish life.

Of course, qualitative values tend to be more debatable than quantitative ones. That coyotes kill ground squirrels is still a more convincing argument for their existence than their beauty is. To many people, sheep ranchers included, coyotes are not beautiful. They aren't always beautiful even to me. It's interesting how much wider a range of emotion a real animal in the wild can evoke than a filmed or caged one. Coyotes tend to look kind of cute in films—bright-eyed and bushy-tailed, as the saying goes. Along the craggy, shaggy old Eel River, they can look pretty rapacious, like highly resourceful killers, which of course they are. But then, there's a beauty in rapacity and resourcefulness too, in a gnawed deer rib cage on a sun-baked gravel bar.

A good, long look at any hunting predator can make you glad there aren't too many of them at the same time it makes you marvel at their strength and grace. Fortunately, the biosphere decrees that predators always must be rare in relation to prey. There always are more plant-eaters than there are meat-eaters because plants are the basic form of food. The prey controls the predator because it is closer to the source of life. A predator capable of exterminating its prey soon would be an extinct predator. It's not easy for a coyote to catch a gopher or jack rabbit. I've seen them try; I haven't seen them succeed. (I watched one coyote in British Columbia that seemed to be having trouble enough catching a butterfly.) There has to be a lot of prey around so that the hard-working predator occasionally can hit the jackpot. One of the reasons the coyote is common is its willingness to take a wide variety of prey. Less adaptable species such as the mountain lion, which preys mostly on deer, can be ghostly in their rarity. I've lived four years among one of the densest lion populations in California, and I haven't seen one.

If there is one quality I value most in the mountain lion, in fact, it is rarity. Lions may be useful in pruning deer populations, promoting deer eugenics, and adorning the landscape, but none of these things excites me quite as much as the thought, every time I go into the hills, that *this* might be the time I finally run across one. Cotton Mather would have found this frivolous, but I don't think it is. Our inquiring primate minds need the novelty and stimulation of rarity. We need to feel that there is more to the world than we know.

# The Mind of the Beaver

ONE of my early memories is of walking across a frozen Connecticut pond with a friend and his father and coming upon a conical mound of sticks. When my friend's father told us it was a beaver lodge, I was fascinated. The snow-covered pond and bare woods seemed more alive because of this evidence of hidden, furry swimmers beneath the ice. I took a stick from the lodge home and kept it in my closet for years, occasionally taking it out to look at the tooth marks on the dry, gray wood. They seemed to promise new worlds to discover beyond the routines of schoolwork and suburban chores.

No wild animal has been a greater incitement to the discovery of new worlds than the beaver. North America was largely explored by men seeking to profit from an insatiable European market for felt hats made from shorn and pressed beaver fur. The Hudson's Bay Company, established in 1669 to trade with the Indians for beaver pelts, was the effective government of most of Canada from the French and Indian War until the mid-nineteenth century. American beaver traders such as Jedediah Smith preceded gold miners and settlers to the West Coast by several decades. During the height of the beaver trade, after the steel trap began to be produced industrially and before new felt-making processes depressed the price of a beaver pelt by some 80 percent, a beaver trapper could average a daily income estimated at thirty-two times that of a farm laborer. It's no wonder that mountain men explored every watershed from Santa Fe to Vancouver in the 1820s. Even after beaver prices fell in the 1840s, an estimated 500,000 beavers were being killed every year, primarily for their fur, which was (and is) used to make coats and collars.

Beaver trappers generally discovered more about geography than they did about beavers. It is one thing to catch a beaver in a trap or deadfall, another to discern its way of life. Beavers were a subject of lively scientific and popular interest in Colonial days, but early beaver lore was based as much on hearsay and imagination as on observation. Writing on the eve of the American Revolution, Captain Jonathan Carver described how, "after mature deliberation," troops of two or three hundred beavers assembled to build dams; how they plastered their dams with "a kind of mortar . . . laid on with their tails;" and how they built their "cabins . . . on poles." This anthropomorphized picture, in which beavers seemed more like a pond-dwelling tribe of people than wild animals, was repeated in dozens of accounts and illustrations, some of which showed beaver lodges with square-frame windows and second stories. The American historian George Bancroft considered beavers superior to Indians in cleanliness, thrift, industry, and architectural skill.

Beavers do have many traits that, viewed from a human standpoint, seem admirable. They spend a lot of time grooming, although their purpose is as much to waterproof their fur with oil as it is to keep clean. They are family animals, generally mating for life; and they are protective of their young, which remain with the parents until two years old. Where food is abundant, large beaver colonies grow up, consisting of many families that coexist peacefully in separate but neighboring quarters. These beaver towns may have evolved as a way of guarding against wolves, otters, bobcats, and other natural predators, although they proved a liability when trappers became the beavers' most deadly predator.

The high regard in which beavers came to be held collided with the fur trade in the late nineteenth century. Beavers were rapidly disappearing from the United States as trappers competed for the last scattered populations. Complete extinction was predicted, and a beaver preservation movement, comparable to the present campaign to save the whales, grew up. The beaver was seen as a paragon of wilderness virtue. Former trappers such as Joseph Henry Taylor and Gray Owl wrote books deploring the beaver trade and romanticizing their own exploits in it. Naturalists, particularly Arthur Dugmore (*The Romance of the Beaver,* 1914) and Enos Mills (*The Beaver World,* 1913), made the first detailed studies of beaver life.

What the naturalists discovered did not have the science-fiction glamour of Colonial accounts, but in a way it was equally extraordinary. Beavers are rodents, the largest in North America, reaching a length of more than four feet, including the tail, and a weight of more than eighty pounds. But they still have rodent brains, which are not particularly large and which lack the abundant convolutions that characterize human (and dolphin) brains. (Brain convolutions are believed to be a sign of intelligence because they increase the surface area of the cerebrum, where thinking is supposed to occur.) Yet Dugmore and Mills watched beavers do things that seemed to require considerable foresight. When their dams were threatened by high water, beavers promptly opened spillways or built smaller dams downstream to relieve the pressure of the fast current. Beavers dug canals as much as 1,000 feet long to divert an extra stream into their pond or to reach a source of food (beavers eat the inner bark of aspens, maples, willows, and other trees). If the canals were dug on sloping terrain, the beavers built small check dams at intervals along them so the water wouldn't flow too fast. Mills quoted Alexander Majors, the originator of the Pony Express, as saying often that beavers "had more engineering skill than the entire Corps of Engineers who were connected with General Grant's army when he besieged Vicksburg."

Before I read Mills and Dugmore, I saw a beaver canal in a marsh along the Stillwater River in Montana's Beartooth–Absaroka Wilderness. It was so straight and tidy, the spoil piled along its bank as if by a dredge, that I didn't think beavers could have made it, although the river was full of beavers. I thought the Forest Service had sent a crew to dig a canal through the marsh, although I couldn't imagine why, since it was a day's walk from a road. Beavers kept puzzling me on that trip. I had conventional notions of low beaver dams across gentle New England streams, with lodges in the centers of ponds. But the Montana beavers had adapted their engineering works to the steep ruggedness of the Beartooth Mountains. I found a large beaver lodge in a dry gully right beside the trail. The only explanation for this I could think of was that the gully might be flooded in winter, which is when beavers live in lodges. (They spend warm weather "on vacation," wandering about and eating water plants.) I passed another gully that looked as though it had been terraced by Asian rice farmers. A series of beaver dams ran as far as I could see up the gully, so that it contained no longer a stream but a string of quiet ponds. Some of the dams were considerably taller than I am, reminding me of miniature Grand Coulees. This terracing presumably made it easier for beavers to ascend the gully and bring back aspens from farther up the mountainside.

Canals are considered the most striking examples of beaver ingenuity because they seem to require more planning than anything else beavers do. They usually appear to have some definite objective, making it unlikely that the beavers could simply be carrying on instinctive, unplanned activity in building them. Dugmore noted that, when they dig a canal to a grove of food trees, beavers build the canal *before* they cut the trees. The canal is thus not dug inadvertently while the beavers are going back and forth to cut and haul trees. It is built with an apparently conscious intention of providing access to a planned "timber sale." That is not to say that there isn't an instinctive element in beaver canal-building. Most aquatic rodents make canallike paths as they move about their territories; but other rodents don't deliberately divert streams with their canals, and they don't build locks in their canals if they happen to be on sloping ground.

There are other examples of beaver "thinking." Enos Mills, who spent twenty-seven years watching beavers, described several ways that a beaver's tree-cutting can show foresight: "He occasionally endeavors to fell trees in a given direction. . . .

He avoids cutting those entangled at the top. . . . Sometimes he will, on a windy day, fell trees on the leeward side of the grove. . . . He commonly avoids felling trees in the heart of the grove, but cuts on the outskirts of it." Mills also saw beavers display just the opposite of this sagacity, cutting trees that were entangled at the top, or in the heart of a grove, so the trees were impossible to move. He found dead beavers that had felled trees on top of themselves. Individually stupid behavior doesn't prove lack of intelligence in a species, though; otherwise, *Homo sapiens* would have to change its scientific name. Indeed, the fact that some beavers are incompetent tree-fellers suggests that tree felling involves thoughtful as well as instinctive behavior. If it were a purely instinctive activity, then all beavers should do it equally well. Wide variation in complex behavior implies a capacity for learning and innovating.

The dam and lodge building that so impressed Colonial writers requires less foresight than canal-building and tree-felling. Like many rodents, beavers are compulsive pilers of sticks during nesting and food-storing. Lodges may have evolved from piles of sticks raised for protection over the stream bank holes that ancestral beavers lived in (and that modern beavers revert to if heavily persecuted or if living along rivers too big to dam). Such primitive dens probably evolved gradually into full-fledged lodges as beavers dug their burrows on small islands or on banks that were seasonally flooded. A beaver lodge is essentially an artificial island with a burrow in it (or several burrows: early explorers found beaver apartment houses—giant lodges with dozens of burrows, accommodating several families).

Dams may have evolved from the beaver's habit of storing cut branches underwater for a winter food supply. (Such storage assures that the bark will not decay, but will remain nutritious throughout the winter.) Dams are not built of whole trees felled across a stream, as some Colonial writers thought, but of many limbs set parallel to the current with their butt ends facing upstream, so their branches interlace and hold the limbs firmly to the stream bottom. That method of anchoring the dam may have begun as a way of assuring that the winter's food supply wouldn't be swept away. Beavers that made food piles big enough to slow or dam their stream might have had better survival rates in the artificial ponds they thus created, and might then have passed on a predilection for such piles to their young. That is all conjecture, of course. We have no way of knowing how beaver dams evolved. Dams and lodges are more a part of the beaver's normal biological activities than canals, though, so they seem less planned and rational.

Even if dam and lodge building are largely instinctive activities, however, they show a great deal of individual variation. Some beavers, especially young or solitary old ones, are sloppy and perfunctory builders. Beavers don't always choose the best possible sites for dams. They'll even build dams where it's obvious that none is required—for example, when they are transplanted to already-existing ponds. On the other hand, dams often are sited as though the best engineering techniques had been used. Beavers have also been known to build lodges over springs, a sagacious way of eliminating the danger that the water at the lodge's entrance might freeze, shutting the resident beavers inside to die of slow starvation. And beavers generally take excellent care of their dams and lodges, plastering them with mud (although not by using their tails as trowels, as Captain Carver thought) and promptly repairing damage, as though mindful that the continued value of property depends on good maintenance.

The likeliest conclusion that I can draw from all this evidence is that beavers are animals with minds, animals that think. They seem to confront their environment in a conscious, deliberate way: they plan, they choose, they solve problems.

An experimental scientist might spend an entire career, or more, on the mysteries of beaver psychology. If the beaver thinks, then *how* does it think? We humans think with language. We can't build dams or canals without it. There's no evidence that beavers have language, though; they're quiet creatures, even for wild animals. They do make various communicative noises, including the well-known tail slap on the water, but such noises don't seem complex enough to communicate canal-building techniques. The sloppy dam-building of young beavers suggests that engineering techniques may be passed down somehow from parents to young, perhaps simply by the young beavers' watching their parents. We don't know enough about beavers to be sure about that, thought. Mills saw little evidence of leadership when he watched groups of beavers at work, although he noted one instance in which parents accompanied their maturing offspring to a new location, helped them build a dam and lodge, and then returned to their old pond, leaving the youngsters in the new one.

Whether beaver "thinking" is handed down from generation to generation or simply occurs in individuals as an adjunct to instinctive behavior, it has had a long time to evolve, much longer than human intelligence. The beaver's first ancestors appeared in the Oligocene Epoch, some 35 million years ago, and the genus *Castor*, to which the modern beaver belongs, was fully developed by the Pliocene Epoch, which began 13 million years ago. During the Ice Age, giant beavers up to nine feet long lived in North American rivers. Assuming (as is not necessarily the case) that these giant beavers had giant beaver brains, I wonder what kind of engineering feats they may have accomplished? They evidently built lodges, since fossil mounds of willow poles capable of housing giant beavers have been unearthed.

Of course, my conclusion that the beaver has a mind isn't the only possible one. An instinct-versus-intelligence controversy has raged around the beaver since modern science discovered it. Baron Cuvier, the early-nineteenth-century French anatomist, "proved" that beavers are purely instinctive creatures by raising baby beavers in isolation. Cuvier claimed that the isolated beavers demonstrated all the talents and abilities of wild beavers. I don't know if Cuvier's beavers built 1,000-foot-long canals complete with check dams to divert entire streams. It seems unlikely they'd have had much scope to do so in captivity. Even if they did, though, that wouldn't necessarily prove that they weren't thinking as they built their canals. It would prove only that they built them without having learned how from other beavers. Cuvier was judging his beavers in anthropomorphic terms. Human intelligence depends heavily on cultural conditioning for its development; people who are raised in isolation, such as the so-called wolf children of India, remain subhuman in behavior, unable to use language or other tools. But that doesn't prove that there couldn't be another kind of intelligence, less dependent on cultural conditioning. After all, no amount of education can turn a truly stupid human into a good engineer. Intelligence requires innate capacity as well as learning.

One has only to spend a little time watching beavers to sense that, rational or not, these are sharp animals. I've never been able to catch beavers off guard, as I've sometimes caught muskrats. Beavers go about their business as I watch, seemingly oblivious of me; but if I begin to edge into a position that might give me an advantage over them, the beavers are gone. Muskrats, on the other hand, bumble right up to my feet as I stand beside their den holes, then panic when they realize they're not alone, tumbling comically into the water.

Beavers seem able to adapt to the worst that humans can do to land. Once while hiking the lunar landscape of an Ohio strip mine, I came upon an eroded, muddy gully that beavers had improved in much the same way that they'd treated the rocky gully in the Beartooth Mountains. They had built a series of check dams across the gully, turning it into a string of pools instead of an eroded watercourse. The fact that the water was opaque with mud and yellowboy (residual sulfur from the coal seam) hadn't stopped them. It was confusing to come upon something as "natural" as beaver dams in such a ravaged landscape.

The beaver's activity on strip-mined land is valued because it reduces erosion and water pollution. Sediment settles behind beaver dams instead of choking rivers. Strip-mining companies prohibit beaver trapping on their land. Of course, the beavers aren't working to conserve soil; they're simply trying to survive in what must be a challenging, if not harsh, environment for them. But that they are surviving, as they've survived the 300-year war that civilization has waged on them, is at least partly a measure of their ingenuity. It might not be so easy to exterminate beavers. While visiting France, after having been told by his hosts that beavers had been extinct in their region for many years, Enos Mills found a piece of beaver-chewed wood in the River Seine.

Accounts of beaver wisdom sometimes challenge belief. There are reports that beavers may learn to spring traps with sticks, and in fact there have been beaver populations that proved virtually untrappable. Trappers believed that beavers could forecast the weather, could predict whether winters would be mild or severe. Mills and Dugmore both failed to see evidence of that, and I'm more inclined to believe them than the trappers. Still, who can say what a mode of thought so different from our own might preceive?

I certainly don't pretend to know how beavers think. We understand little enough about how our own gray matter produces canals and dams. Scientific attention has shifted from the question of beaver intelligence to that of whale and dolphin intelligence, partly because whales have big, convoluted brains like ours, partly because we are in danger of exterminating them, as we were in danger of exterminating the beaver 100 years ago. Whales certainly deserve our attention. I sometimes think, though, that our shifting interest in various animals reflects our vanity as well as our concern. We wanted to save the beaver because it builds dams, lodges, and canals—as we do. Now we want to save the whales because they have big brains and (possibly) language—as we do. But there are many things deserving our attention that are quite unlike us. The beaver's solitary, silent way of thinking may be one of them.

# The Madtom, the Wood Rat
# and the Riffle Shell

IT may come as a surprise to zoo-goers and "Wild Kingdom" watchers that there at least thirty-four endangered species in or near the Greater Columbus, Ohio, area, and quite a few more across the state as a whole. Some of them are quite spectacular, including the river otter, bobcat, bald eagle, and paddlefish (a river fish reaching a length of six feet). However, large rare animals are usually just wanderers or migrants. In heavily populated Ohio, the typical endangered species are small, inconspicuous animals with specialized habitat needs—creatures whose disappearance from the biosphere might not be attended with even much of a whimper.

Yet, in a modest way, these creatures are as interesting and significant as tigers, rhinoceroses, and the other majestic fauna of zoo cages and television sets. We just generally know less about them.

Virtually nothing is known about the life history of the Scioto madtom, a dimunitive, gray and white catfish found nowhere in the world outside central Ohio. When it was included in the U.S. Endangered Species List in 1975, the media gave it nationwide coverage. But what can you say about a creature that has only been found three times, and that hasn't been seen alive since 1957?

The name *madtom* derives from a peculiar aspect of these fishes' anatomy. Small sacs of poisonous fluid at the base of pectoral spines just behind the head and on each side of the body can deliver the effect of a bee sting to unwary handlers if the spine pierces the skin and the poison is injected. Like other catfishes, madtoms can erect these spines and lock them in place, making themselves quite a mouthful for larger fishes. They are nonetheless a favorite food for bass. There are twenty-five other madtom species, all quite similar in appearance to the Scioto madtom. It is distinguished from them by details of its fins and skeleton. The 2.2-inch length of the largest Scioto madtom on record makes it one of the smaller madtoms, although there may be hundred-pound individuals for all we know.

Presumably, the Scioto madtom also resembles its relatives in behavior, resting in holes during the day and foraging on clean stream bottoms at night. Madtoms find food by touch, using taste buds on their fins and bodies to find out if something is edible. (They are rather easy to fool and will cheerfully eat pebbles soaked in beef juice.) They eat mostly small insects. Globular masses of eggs are laid under stones, where the male guards them. During this time, the male's head becomes enlarged and blackish, which helps to camouflage him when he peeks out from under his stone. After the eggs hatch, the male herds the tiny madtoms until they are about a centimeter long. If alarmed, they may take refuge in his mouth. All this is merely speculation where the Scioto madtom is concerned, however. The species is too scarce to have been studied in the wild.

Dr. Milton Trautman, professor emeritus of zoology at Ohio State University, discovered the Scioto madtom in 1943. It was found again in 1944 before its last appearance in 1957. All specimens were found in the same fifteen-foot-square section of Big Darby Creek in Pickaway County. Specimens were found only during the fall, which may mean the madtoms spend the rest of the year somewhere else. Nobody has any idea where. The fact that the last specimens were found twenty years ago doesn't mean that the species is extinct, although this is possible. It is more likely that Scioto madtoms exist in such small numbers that the chances of encountering one are very low. Trautman had been studying and collecting Big Darby's fishes for eighteen years before he found the first Scioto madtom. "I think there's a greater chance of an automobile coming down stream and hitting us from behind than there is of catching a madtom," Trautman told a newspaper reporter who interviewed him while he was seining the stream in the summer of 1975. "That's why, when I'm working the stream, I always look behind me."

Trautman is worried about the future of many freshwater fishes: "A third of the fishes of Ohio are endangered, really." He opens his definitive work *The Fishes of Ohio,* and lists forty-eight central Ohio fishes he considers threatened to some degree, including the pumpkinseed sunfish, Ohio muskellunge, and yellow bullhead. All, the Scioto madtom included, are threatened by destruction of their natural habitat. The madtom is more threatened than most because its range is so restricted. It could become extinct almost overnight if Big Darby Creek's bottom was covered with silt from activities such as dam-building or channel-dredging upstream. The silt would cut off its food supply and smother its eggs.

The fact that the Scioto madtom has survived until now is perhaps something of an anomaly in Ohio, where the vast number of streams have been drastically modified (or have simply dried up) in the past hundred years. Big Darby Creek is an exception, not having been to any great extent channelized, dammed, or polluted. It still contains a substantial number of species, an ecological index of a habitat's health and stability. One hundred of Ohio's 166 known fish species have been found in Big Darby, a diversity of which any tropical reef would be proud to boast. Trautman and his students collected ninety species in a short stretch that includes the Scioto madtom's little domain. Two dams are currently proposed for Big Darby.

Trautman considers it quite possible that the Scioto madtom will show up again if Big Darby is left unmolested. Unusually favorable spawning conditions in the future could result in a miniscule population explosion of the species, as occurred in 1957. Fourteen were located that year, a veritable army of Scioto madtoms.

Most of central Ohio's endangered species are not as rare or as mysterious as the Scioto madtom. Residents of the area are probably familiar with a characteristic trait of one endangered mammal, although they may be unaware that it lives here. This is the Allegheny or eastern wood rat, a close relative of the pack rat of Western lore. The Allegheny wood rat shares with its western cousins a compulsion to arrange and rearrange objects, which may lead it to abscond with coins, eyeglasses, keys, and other things of value to humans, leaving in their place twigs, nuts, or other things of presumable value to wood rats. Of course, wood rats are not motivated by any feelings of fairness when they "trade" objects; they simply put down whatever they happen to be carrying when they find something more interesting.

Nobody knows exactly why the Allegheny wood rat has become endangered in Ohio. It is still somewhat common in Kentucky, Missouri, and other states. A probable reason is that there is very little undisturbed habitat in Ohio of the type the wood rat needs. Allegheny wood rats usually live in forested, hilly country with cliffs and rock outcroppings. Most of the land that fits this description in Ohio was intensively farmed until the 1930s, and the wood rats that had lived there may have been starved out by overgrazing or decimated by farm cats.

Just the word *rat* is repulsive to many people, but the Allegheny wood rat is Dr. Jekyll to the Norway rat's Mr. Hyde. It only superficially resembles the scaly-tailed, filthy Norway rat of our slums and garbage dumps, and comes from an entirely different line of evolution, the New World rodents. This group includes the pretty little deer mice found throughout North America. The wood rat, in fact, looks like a giant deer mouse, with lustrous black eyes, large ears, white underparts and feet, and a silky-furred tail. In behavior, it is about as close to being a perfect gentleman as any wild animal (discounting, of course, its kleptomaniacal qualities). It prefers a quiet, retired life in a nest of sticks, which it builds in caves or, sometimes, trees. The nests are often quite large, as high as six feet, and may be inhabited by lizards, tree frogs, mice, or other uninvited guests that the wood rat proprietor tolerates. Separate areas are maintained for food storage, trash, and excreta. Wood rats appear to be almost entirely vegetarian, subsisting on a frugal diet of fern stems, poison ivy leaves, and a wide variety of other wild plants. They have been observed spreading herbs on rocks to dry in the sun for winter storage.

Even when disturbed, wood rats are rather easy-going. They seldom squeal or rush about hysterically as do other rodents such as chipmunks. Demonstrations of aggressiveness are usually confined to stamping the hind feet or rattling the tail against the sticks of the nest. This produces a sound oddly reminiscent of the flapping of roll-up window blinds. In California, where nests of the dusky-footed wood rat are common, nocturnal woodlands sometimes sound like skid row hotels full of Peeping Toms. Wood rats do tend to squabble with one another (they stand up on their hind legs and spar with their front paws); but since they prefer to live alone, such conflicts arise much less regularly than among the gregarious Norway rats, for whom gang warfare, murder, and cannibalism are almost a norm.

Dennis Case, nongame biologist for the Ohio Division of Wildlife, says that wood rats remain calm even when caught in a live trap, a situation that understandably causes most animals to panic. Case is conducting a study of wood rats to learn where they still live in the state, and to investigate the possibility of reestablishing them in a few places. The largest Ohio population is apparently in Adams County, where wood rats are also known as tobacco rats because they sometimes enter the lowlands and make off with tobacco leaves for an unknown purpose—to use as food, nest material (or to feed a nicotine habit?). There are some in Athens County, and there may be a few in Fairfield and Hocking counties. The first museum specimen of the Allegheny wood rat in Ohio was found in Hocking County in 1923 on land that eventually will be part of the Columbus Metropolitan Park District.

One of the wood rats captured in the Wildlife Division study was temporarily detained for some portrait studies by Al Staffan, Ohio Department of Natural Resources photographer, before being returned to the wild. Probably a juvenile, it was a very engaging creature indeed, alert and curious, with soft, grayish-brown fur, neat white paws, and exceptionally long, sensitive-looking nose whiskers. It was clean, had no smell, and hardly made a sound as it moved about its cage, although sudden noises caused it to wince and stamp its hind feet. Strange hands introduced into the cage elicited only a few sedate sniffs and gentle, exploratory nibbles. Staffan's only complaint was that the wood rat had rubbed the fur off the top of its nose peering between the cage wires, giving it a somewhat unphotogenic appearance.

American Indians esteemed wood rats for their apparently tender and delicious flesh—this raises the topic of usefulness, which usually comes up sooner or later in relation to endangered species. Too often the obvious fact that madtoms, wood rats, and many other threatened animals have no clear economic value is used as an excuse for minimizing or ignoring the considerable ecological, scientific, and aesthetic value they do have, not to mention their potential value if we can refrain from burying them. In any case, economic uselessness is not a requirement for endangered species. One of the more useful groups of animals in Ohio is among the most threatened.

Many people with an interest in natural history or wild foods may have heard vague mention of freshwater clams, but the subject somehow never seems as pertinent as clams and oysters from the seacoast hundreds of miles away. This is unfortunate, because Ohio is (or was) a globally significant treasury of freshwater mollusks. One early naturalist reported so many new species of freshwater mollusks here that his colleagues in Europe began to wonder about him. He was right though. At that time there were in Ohio at least seventy-eight species of naiades—bivalves named after the river nymphs of Greek mythology because they aren't quite the same as oysters, mussels, or clams. Today, fifty-nine of these species survive, sixteen of them on the Ohio endangered list, several on the U.S. list. The rest are extirpated or extinct.

Naiades resemble clams but lack the "neck" many clams use in burrowing into tidal mud and sand. Both groups pull themselves about with a muscular "foot," unlike oysters and mussels, which spend most of their lives attached to rocks. Various naiad species reach sizes comparable to commercial clams and oysters, and are just as nourishing. It's doubtful that anyone eats naiades now because of pollution, but they were a major food of the Ohio Indians. From about 6000 to 1500 B.C. they were apparently *the* major food judging from huge piles of naiad shells found along many rivers. The sophisticated Adena and Hopewell peoples used naiad shells for beads and utensils, and also treasured the superior pearls that naiades produce. Later cultures also used naiad shells as hide-scrapers and hoes.

White settlers ate naiades and fed them to pigs at the same time they were probably decimating naiad populations by cutting down the forest to plant crops. Muddy runoff from plowed fields may have smothered thousands of naiad populations that had evolved in harmony with clear wilderness streams. In the late nineteenth century, a booming industry grew up around buttons made from the lovely, durable, often delicately colored mother-of-pearl on the inside of naiad shells. Hundreds of thousands of tons of living naiades were dredged up, steamed out, and shipped to button factories. Eventually, depletion of naiad stocks from pollution, habitat destruction, and the industry's heedless harvesting activities more or less wiped out the mother-of-pearl button, which was replaced by glass or plastic buttons. Naiades languished unexploited for some years, with some restoration of their populations.

Then the Japanese cultured pearl industry became interested in American naiades. Cultured pearls are traditionally grown in oysters, but a small bead of foreign matter must be implanted in the oyster's living tissues to start the pearl-making process. Naiad shells are ideal for these beads, and the Japanese supply, which had been coming from China's rivers, was cut off when that country went communist. Naiades are still being harvested for this purpose today. Dr. David Stansbery, a malacologist and director of the Ohio State University Museum of Zoology, wonders if this can continue for much more than a decade, however. Stansbery suspects that the rate of naiad habitat destruction from channel-dredging, impoundments, urbanization of watersheds, and other factors is accelerating too quickly to allow much more time for any mollusk-based industry to be economically feasible. Meanwhile, he notes, the Japanese are thinking of moving their entire cultured pearl industry over here to cut down on transportation costs. In this case, pearls would be grown in naiades instead of oysters. The colorful, iridescent pearls that naiades produce are gaining in popularity over solid white oyster pearls. (It is believed that Julius Caesar invaded Britain partly to secure a supply of freshwater naiad pearls, of which the vain conquerer was inordinately fond.)

The humble naiades may seem dull, spending their lives filtering organic detritus from the water as they lie among the river rocks, which they superficially resemble. Their life cycle is rather fascinating though. Individual naiades are either male or female. Some species have differently shaped shells according to their sex. During breeding, males release sperm into the water, which is drawn into the incurrent apertures (mouths) of downstream females. Fertilized eggs develop as embryos called glochidia and are kept in specialized structures on the mother's gills until ready for the next phase in the naiad life cycle. Glochidia are bivalved specks whose single ability, once released into the water, is to snap shut on the gill or fin of a fish. This accomplished, the glochidium becomes encysted in the tissues of the host fish, and slowly digests the cells upon which it shut.

Glochidia of each naiad species apparently parasitize particular kinds of fishes (or other aquatic animals). They do little harm in the process. Sometimes, "tricks" serve to draw the host close enough for the glochidia to climb aboard. Females of some naiad species discharge their glochidia in mucous sheaths that resemble worms or newly-hatched fishes. A bass or sunfish biting the sheath would get a mouthful of glochidia. Other species possess a curious structure called a mantle flap that is shaped and colored like a pair of small fish. It even has dark, eye-like spots. The mantle flap projects into the river current, undulating fishily, and probably attracting larger fish. A predaceous fish striking at it would cause the naiad to close quickly, squirting glochidia-laden water into the fish's mouth.

Most glochidia only remain on the host a few weeks. They don't grow larger, but develop internally. The "foot," heart, gill buds, digestive tube, and other organs are formed; and when the juvenile naiad drops off the host, it is able to pull itself

about. Most juveniles succumb to various environmental haz-
ards. Those that survive grow rather quickly until they reach
sexual maturity, then growth slows down. Naiad age can be read
from annual growth rings on the shell. Thin-shelled species may
live from four to ten years; thick-shelled species may have a
twenty- to forty-year life span. Some individuals are reported to
have lived almost a century.

Stansbery estimates that there are three endangered naiad species in rivers and creeks of the Columbus vicinity. One of these,
a small brownish naiad called the Simpson's shell, may have
been extirpated by the Alum Creek dam, which was built virtually on top of the only known population in central Ohio. The
Simpsons' shell lives under rocks and parasitizes, not fishes, but
a large, gilled salamander called the mud puppy. They may still
live in Big Darby Creek or the Olentangy River, but they are
probably so scarce now that specimens are unlikely to be found.

The club shell is known to live in Big Darby Creek and possibly in the Olentangy. It is medium-sized, with an amber shell
decorated with an intricate pattern of viridian rays. (Naiad
shells have river colors—yellows, greens, ochres, and browns—
instead of the showy blues and reds on the outsides of sea shells.
But they are beautiful in a subtle way. The algae and mud of the
river must be cleaned off before the colors become visible.) As
with most naiad species, nobody knows what fishes are involved
in the club shell life cycle. It is not known to be reproducing in
central Ohio, since juvenile shells haven't been found. This
means, of course, that conditions in the streams may no longer
be tolerable for this species, and it may disappear when adults
now living die. Nobody knows why club shells aren't reproducing. A change in river chemistry from a new sewage treatment
plant or a change in water temperature from a new reservoir
upstream can be enough to wipe out numerous species adapted
to more natural stream conditions. Technology for monitoring
and controlling human changes of the environment is still in the
horse and buggy stage, and will probably remain there unless
there is some reordering of priorities.

The northern riffle shell is still breeding in Big Darby Creek,
another beneficiary of that stream's relatively natural state. It

also inhabits the same general portion of the stream as the Scioto madtom. The riffle shell is greenish-ochre in color and inhabits sandy riffles. (A riffle is an area where the water surface is broken.) This is one of the sexually dimorphic species. Shells of females are rounded; those of males are pointed and grooved. Judging from the widely separated growth rings on the specimens in the Ohio State University Museum of Zoology, the riffle shell is a fast-growing species. This may help explain its persistence.

Scientists are discovering that naiad shell growth rings can indicate a good deal more than age and growth rate. Metals are excreted into the annual shell layers, indicating the concentrations of pollutants such as lead and mercury in stream water year after year. Naiades also collect pesticides and other toxic pollutants in their tissues, making them a promising vehicle for monitoring the quantities of poisons we dribble into our waterways. Such new and potential uses are certainly the most compelling reason for trying to save endangered species. We may need them more than we know.

Every living species has an unbelievably complex genetic makeup that differs very much from that of even its closest relatives. This is lost forever when extinction occurs. As Trautman points out, there may be a substance in the Scioto madtom's liver that could cure cancer. Certainly, nobody can say there isn't such a substance, since there aren't enough Scioto madtom livers around to study. We would have to wait for the next madtom population surge in an undammed, unchannelized Big Darby Creek for that. This may seem like wild talk, but the assertion that an obscure and pestiferous blue *Penicillium* mold would bring about the development of antibiotics might have seemed pretty wild fifty years ago.

# Starlings

THE heather on the low hills and the reeds and sphagnum mosses in the bogs were pale from frost in the first light of morning. They formed a thin layer over the jumble of stones and clay that the retreating continental icesheet had dumped there not very long before. It was November, and the few remaining songbirds were silent in the circular groves of birch trees that dotted the hills. Then, as the sky reddened, a sound began to rise from the bog. It was not the counterpoint of songs and cries that is usually associated with birds; there was something monolithic and relentless about it. It rose from a whisper to a whistling roar in a startlingly short time. A deeper note, the sound of wings, arose as hundreds of blackish, short-tailed birds streamed from the reeds and willow thickets, landing among the heather and grasses of the hillside like a hail of darts. As they opened their sharp beaks to sing, the feathers on their heads and necks erected, giving them a ruffled and crested appearance. Their plumage was a peculiar glazing of ochre specks over violet-green irridescence. A falcon soared over the ridge, but they paid no attention. Nor did he, knowing from experience that a descent into the swarm would end in confusion and empty talons.

Suddenly, the birds rose from the hillside. The hail of darts coalesced as it rose and became a pulsating sphere, then an oval as the flock moved swiftly up the valley. There is nothing in nature to match the amorphous elegance of a flock of starlings. Other species display more color or grace when they flock, but starlings are unexcelled in rippling coordination. They are like gymnasts who begin lying face down on the floor and then proceed to flip themselves over it in every direction and posture without ever taking a definite stance. Or imagine a giant amoeba, freed from gravity and incited to dance. Individual birds and small groups left or joined the flock, but it remained a single entity. It flickered strangely as the birds banked and swerved. In the distance, it was a living smudge against the sky, sometimes dark, at times almost invisible.

A herd of aurochs was grazing among the hills. Five thousand years later, Julius Caesar described these wild oxen as being the size of a small elephant. The last one died in 1621. A grove stood on top of one of the hills, and the starlings came wheeling in, settled into it momentarily so that the birds on one side of the flock were taking off as the birds on the other side were alighting, then circled the herd. Abruptly, the smudge became a thundercloud as each bird angled its wings, and spread its tailfeathers. Then the cloud flattened down in a dense low mist that billowed and rolled as the oxen disturbed it by starting or snorting. The starlings ran nimbly about the aurochs' legs, picking through the fresh manure for seeds and the larvae of internal parasites. Many fluttered onto the broad, shaggy backs and combed the hair for insects that found shelter there.

The herd was a great convenience for the birds, whose summer fare of insects was killed off or driven underground. The starlings probably contributed to the health and comfort of the herd. After a few hours of feeding, most of the flock fanned out into the hills to forage for wild fruit, but stayed in the vicinity of the wandering herd and came back to feed again when the sun was low, not a very long time in the Baltic autumn. By sunset, the flock was back at the same hillside it had left in the morning. The birds that had branched off during the day also returned. Then a high arching funnel of birds formed between the hillside and the marsh, and, in a while, there was not a bird visible. When the stars came out, incredibly brilliant in the northern sky, the roost had faded into silence.

Snow fell during the night, and some of the birds began to move on to roosts farther south. Their place was taken by birds from north of the Baltic, and it was not until winter, when the snow lay deep and crusted and even the aurochs retreated into the forests, that the roost was abandoned. The flocks passed on to the marshes of southern Europe, or across the Mediterranean to the rich grasslands of what is now the Sahara Desert. Other flocks converged on Egypt and Persia from as far off as Siberia. There they must have had their first taste of orchards and vineyards.

*Sturnus vulgaris,* the common starling, is a member of the avian family Sturnidae, of which most species are rather colorful birds living in Africa or Tropical Asia. The mynah is one of these; like it, the starling is a mimic. How the starling adapted to the more northerly climates is not known, but it was a pretty successful adaptation. A society for the protection of starlings in prehistoric Europe would have complained only of a certain unregulated quality in the world that, if it did not threaten the bird's existence, didn't exactly promote it either. There were the aurochs and bison, but they wandered, often into the deep forests, unfavorable environments for freewheeling starling flocks. The fruits and berries were scattered. For a few thousand years before Christ, things looked dim as a moister climate caused the spread of the dense Hyrcanian oak forests that pushed the Romans to expand across Europe. But this situation was cleared up most gratifyingly as medieval man burned the forest and put the fruit and herds in convenient, concentrated form. Starlings like to nest in tree holes, but roof eaves and chimney pots are acceptable substitutes.

Then, in an unprecedented burst of goodwill, nineteenth-century man exported the species to North and South America, Australia, and New Zealand. The first American starlings nested under the eaves of the American Museum of Natural History in New York in 1891. They were not, as is sometimes said, imported to combat the already pestiferous English sparrows, but for the same sentimental reasons that sparrows were introduced. Their benefactor was an ornithologist and Shakespearean named Scheifflin who decided to bring all the birds mentioned in the bard's work to the new world. The starlings were his only success. It took the enterprising birds a little over seventy years to colonize the continent from Alaska to northern Mexico.

Starlings have demonstrated their ability to thrive in the more polluted or urban environments. They even make pollution themselves, contaminating livestock feed and depositing layers of guano a foot thick under their more populous roosts. A roost in Virginia's Dismal Swamp has been used simultaneously by as many as 20 million birds. And modern agriculture, with its flat, monotonous acres of a single crop is not discouraging to starlings if there is a roosting spot within twenty miles. Every year Sonoma County in California turns more of its acreage into wine grapes. The agricultural commissioner there fears that an early winter in Oregon and Washington, driving flocks down before the grape harvest, could wipe out the crop.

The sky above the rooftops is clammy with early morning fog, but the linnets, robins, and towhees have been singing for half an hour. A starling flutters out from under the dark eaves of the house, perches on the raingutter, and gives a series of low, insinuating whistles. Cedar waxwings are flocking around the holly bush in the backyard. The starling flies down to an ornamental birch tree in the front yard. She picks at the catkins a while, moving around the trunk in a spiral like a woodpecker, then descends to the ground, where her mate joins her.

Their yellow beaks show clearly against the dark earth as they probe among bark chips that have been scattered under some bushes. A month before, in February, their beaks were gray. They turned yellow as the birds' gonads swelled and released testosterone, a hormone that causes a change in pigmentation. Their plumage is much glossier than it was during the winter— the ochre specks that tipped the feathers of their fall molt have worn off, leaving the showy, irridescent parts. The gonads also caused a change in the emotional state of the birds that led them to leave the flock and settle under the eaves of the house. There is another pair of starlings at the next corner of the house; the birds can tolerate a high nesting density, which gives them an advantage in the matter of population increase. Starlings can be violent, crafty usurpers of native, hole-nesting species—

woodpeckers, bluebirds and even sparrow hawks. But these birds have chosen an unoccupied niche.

One of the starlings on the ground picks up a piece of straw, holds it a moment, then drops it absent-mindedly. A car door slams, and they fly up to the TV aerial. They see the other pair bathing in the garage raingutter so they join them with a great splashing. Then the birds all zoom off in different directions. One flies back to the house, hones her beak on the gutter, peers around cautiously and disappears under the eaves. In a while, her mate flies up with a twig in his beak; but the back door of the house opens, and he ducks down into the gutter with it. During the human workday, the starlings are hardly seen at all. They spend their time feeding quietly or performing love rituals in the trees. This unassuming family life is a neat bit of survival engineering—if they nested in flocks they'd be much more vulnerable.

A few weeks later, they are nest-building seriously, methodically bringing pieces of straw up from the backyard. Starling nests are untidy heaps of straw on which they lay, in April, five to seven beautiful green eggs. When these have been hatched and fledged (if an unmated male starling hasn't sneaked in and petulantly thrown the eggs out of the nest), another batch is laid in June. Meanwhile, the first brood forms flocks that will be joined by the parents and second brood later in the summer. That can mean five times as many starlings after the breeding season as before.

For a little while, the pale green glow of the city to the west and the yellow glare of the power plant and gypsum mill across the river obscured the light in the east. Then it began to spread over the sky; the distant hills appeared on the horizon. The river ran between levees, so the rushes and tule reeds of the natural delta occurred only on islands or along the banks. Pheasants called in the harvested croplands behind the levees, and wild geese passed high overhead like sooty cobwebs drifting southward. As the sun rose, red and huge in the haze, a wave of noise came from the marshy islands as thousands of red-winged blackbirds, Brewer's blackbirds, and starlings woke up and flew over the levees, settling onto the fields or the power lines that marched across them. The blackbirds formed scattered, trailing flocks; the starlings larger, denser ones. They billowed and swarmed across the odorous dirt, then moved off toward the hills.

The sun was yellow and bright when the flocks reached the feedlot. It looked odd among the bare brown hills—acres of angular, brightly-painted mixing and storage bins and trampled pens full of steers being fattened for slaughter. The blackbirds scattered over the whole area, feeding mostly on the litter of waste grain, but the starlings were more discriminating. Ignoring the unused pens, they flocked around the feeding troughs and warm manure of the full ones, gobbling the expensive feed, rich in fat and protein, that the cattle being "finished" were given. On that day, the ground of the pens had been sprinkled with chicken-feed pellets that had been dyed blue and treated with a compound called Trichloro-p-toluidine-hydrochloride. The starlings found these attractive, and many ate varying quantities of them.

After a few hours, the flock fanned out into the hills as usual. By late afternoon, birds that had eaten a lot of pellets were crouched on the ground or on fences with their feathers fluffed out as though they were cold, although the California sun was warm enough even in late November. Their blood was running more and more sluggishly as it filled with uric acid from disabled kidneys. The birds began to have trouble breathing, then they lost consciousness and died, without cries or convulsions. The flock fed at the lot again before it returned to the river and funneled back into the roost.

During the night, the birds that had eaten moderate or small amounts of pellets also died. In the morning, after the unaffected birds had flown, the marsh was littered with several thousand dead starlings, a few hundred blackbirds, and two dead crows. Some of the corpses still clung to their perches on bent reeds. A Cooper's hawk swooped down and grabbed one of these. Since the slow-acting poison had been metabolized and excreted by the starling hours before, he suffered no noticeable ill effects from eating it. In a few weeks, most of the dead birds had been replaced by flocks from the north.

# Ravens

ONCE in a while, I'm awakened on a clear winter morning by a sound reminiscent of water gurgling in a drainpipe, and I know that ravens are visiting the English walnut trees in front of the house. I look stealthily through the curtains and perhaps catch a glimpse of a stately black bird strutting across the road. With a beak as heavy and deadly looking as a tomahawk, it is holding a walnut. The situation seems a little incongruous. The beak seems more suited to punching through the stiff hide of a winter-killed deer than to picking nuts, and the bird itself, huge by bird standards, would look more appropriate on some crag or shaggy fir than perched in a front yard. But the ravens are content, or so it seems from their gurgling-drain call, a sound they often make while soaring on a sunny wind.

I haven't been able to see how the ravens crack the walnuts and get the meat out. (They may simply be playing with the nuts, as they play with sticks and stones.) I suppose they would crack a nut as a crow or jay would, by holding it with a foot and hammering it with the beak, although the raven's beak does seem overdeveloped for such a task, as though one were to slice oranges with a saber. Maybe they drop the nuts on roads for cars to crack, as crows have been seen to do with clams. But it's not easy to watch ravens closely in my town in northern California, even though they're an almost daily sight flying overhead or visiting compost piles and vacant lots. They like to keep a few fencerows or oak trees between themselves and the nearest human.

This shyness seems more a matter of policy than of fear. Ravens are not given to hysterias of their relatives in the family Corvidae. The approach of a human does not evoke in them the ostentatious, delighted screeching of jays or the mass panic and flight of crows. Ravens simply make room. Their *kaaa* warning cry seems nonchalant, even bored.

I once watched a raven flock at a winter roost in a pine plantation. There was no problem about my approaching within twenty or thirty feet of them. They discreetly ignored me, and I didn't mind that. There were at least a hundred ravens there—a hundred flying tomahawks—and I was alone in a largely open landscape not too far from where Alfred Hitchcock filmed *The Birds*. But I wasn't allowed any closer than twenty feet; the birds retreated then, keeping a minimum distance. On occasion, ravens have been known to mob people approaching their nests, even to drop stones at climbers near their aeries, but I've seen no records of ravens injuring living humans. Ravens have been enthusiastic feeders at battlefields and gallows, as epic poetry has graphically described, but that is more a commentary on human savagery than on ravens'.

The question of raven savagery is somewhat problematic. Ravens are quite capable of killing animals as large as men. That is not surprising for a bird that has a 50-inch wingspan (comparable to that of large hawks and owls) and that may travel in flocks of more than a hundred. Ravens have been seen killing young seals on polar ice in the following way: one bird flies onto a basking seal's escape hole in the ice, blocking it, while another kills the seal by repeated blows to the head with its beak. Last year, a short article in *The New York Times* reported ravens killing cattle in Ontario in a similar manner, by pecking out their eyes and then dispatching them. Yet unlike eagles, wolves, and coyotes, ravens don't seem to have incurred the wrath of stock raisers. When I asked the agriculture commissioner of a California county about reports of ravens killing newborn lambs, he didn't seem concerned or, for that matter, particularly receptive to the idea of adding yet another "varmint" to the register of agricultural pests he was charged with controlling. Ground squirrels and blackbirds aroused his passions; ravens didn't.

Perhaps ravens are too smart to attack large animals habitually. They may have tomahawk beaks and four-foot wingspans, but bird bones are fragile, and even a sheep has *some* capacity for self-defense. Ravens lack the golden eagle's ability to stun prey with powerful talons and the coyote's ability to attack under cover of darkness. When small animals, or dead ones, are available for food, why bother with large ones? As with most wild creatures, the raven's response to its hazardous environment includes a healthy desire to avoid trouble.

While crows and jays tend to make a noisy game of caution, ravens practice it with quiet calculation. Raven prudence can have mysterious subtleties. Not only did the ravens at the winter roost keep me at a distance, they wouldn't let me watch them with binoculars, either. When I trained the binoculars on an individual bird, it immediately would hop or flap out of my field of vision, not far, just to another branch or tree top, but far enough to escape scrutiny. I don't understand how each individual raven could have known I was focusing on it in particular, but then I don't understand how animals (or people) know when someone is looking at them with the naked eye. The sensitivity of animals to being stared at is enough to make one believe in extrasensory perception. In any case, ravens have superhumanly sharp vision, as with large birds generally, so when they evaded my binoculars they may have been acting on visual data.

Ravens don't make a rigid policy of avoiding human proximity, though. They can be strangely approachable. While walking in the hills north of the Golden Gate one foggy day, I suddenly came within ten feet of two ravens perched on an abandoned corral fence. They did not flee or even acknowledge my presence or that of a black angus calf that was watching them curiously with its moist nose a few inches from the larger raven's feet. They had better things to do. Each raven had caught a rodent, and they neatly butchered and ate their catches as calf and I watched. Each bit off its rodent's head and ate that, then slit open the abdomen with the sharp hook at the end of its beak, removed and discarded the viscera, and finally swallowed the body whole, feet and tail included.

I think the rodents were pocket gophers. I had seen ravens catch rodents in that heavily grazed area by diving suddenly to the ground, and pocket gophers coming up nearsightedly to push earth out of their burrows seemed the likely victims of such a maneuver on that terrain. The rodents seemed too large to be field voles, the other likely candidates. Descriptions of ravens catching and eating rodents aren't common, so I was a little surprised to see the birds' evident facility at it. Ravens usually are characterized as scavengers, particularly in the far north, where they will eat *anything* while under winter stress, including the feces of sled dogs. Still, it's reasonable to assume that birds as clever as ravens will make use of most available food sources, and in fact raven stomach castings have been found to contain ample traces of plant material and insects as well as the carrion that constitutes their main diet.

Crows and jays eat much more vegetable matter than ravens, but aren't averse to eating carrion or to catching small animals, when possible. The duller-witted hawks and eagles occasionally or habitually add carrion to their diets, taking the scavenger role, while vultures will double as predators by catching snakes or other small creatures they can handle with their weak talons. Among large, predatory birds, it seems only owls live entirely on what they catch, and I'm not even sure of them. Hunger is a powerful incentive to versatility.

Perhaps those rodent-eating ravens let me approach so closely simply because they were hungry, in a hurry to fill their stomachs. A gopher is a nice big morsel of fat and protein for a hard-flying bird on a chilly and windy coast. They certainly seemed happy after their meal. The smaller of the two made soft, resonant *craw-craw-craw-craw* sounds, which prompted the larger to flap to the same fence post. They perched close together a moment, rather like two human diners enjoying post-prandial serenity on a restaurant banquette. The smaller raven placed its beak under the larger's, then reached up and gently touched the tip of its beak to the top of the larger's head. Both birds blinked, bluish eye membranes sliding over sharply glittering pupils in a way that seemed curiously vulnerable and sensitive. They became restless then and flew away into the mist.

Ravens at times display themselves with bravado. I was climbing a steep knoll one brilliant spring day when four appeared overhead and began an aerial dance. They circled in the stiff eddies of wind above the knoll, hardly moving their wings, merely ruddering delicately with their wedge-shaped tails. At first, they didn't make a sound, just swept back and forth about 20 feet above me. They climbed, sideslipped, crossed each other's courses, swooped, and climbed again. It was mesmerizing to watch, as though the birds were weaving spells in the blue sky with their shapes like black crosses.

They continued this silent weaving for several moments, and it evidently excited them. The pattern of their flight quickened. One bird croaked several times as though in exhilaration, and the four paired off. Each pair flew in unison, one partner close above the other as they made steep little dives. Pulling out of these dives, the birds made the same gurgling-drain sounds that I hear around my walnut trees. The pairing and diving seemed to complete the performance. Still hardly moving their wings, the ravens soared away on an updraft, vanishing as suddenly as they had appeared.

Ravens probably are the most consciously aerobatic of birds. They can't fly backward like hummingbirds or dive at almost supersonic speeds like falcons and swifts, but they are unsurpassed for general aerial dexterity. I've seen them flying circles around hawks and golden eagles. While the raptors soared in their usual effortless arcs, the ravens made arcs just as effortlessly within those arcs, occasionally rising above the hawks to swoop at them and harass them. The hawks kept circling higher, perhaps to discourage their tormentors, but the ravens stayed with them until the whole troupe faded into the blue. (Even ravens aren't immune to the persecutions of kingbirds and blackbirds, however, and it's amusing to see them dodging and croaking in protest while a half dozen birds about a fifth their size tyrannize them.)

The sky above a raven roost at sunset is like a tentful of trapeze artists. At the pine plantation roost, I watched perhaps fifty

ravens in the air at once, all doing aerobatics. A pair came together, one raven flying above the other for a moment; then the
lower partner flipped onto its back and started flying upside
down. They flew breast to breast for a while then, still in unison, did a roll, dive, and swooping climb almost too quick for
the eye to follow, after which they flew into another group and
changed partners. Nearby, two ravens were trying to fly with the
same partner. One of the rivals dived at the other, which escaped
by doing an aerial somersault and flying away in an opposite
direction. A lone raven carried a stone in one claw, which it
dropped; the bird swooped and caught it in its beak, then
dropped and caught it again. The ravens often let their legs hang
down nonchalantly as they performed these feats, which
brought to mind a human acrobat negligently resting hand on
hip while dancing on a tightrope.

How did ravens arrive at their command of the sky? We don't
know. Humans quite possibly know less about ravens now than
they did 10,000 years ago. Ravens played a large role in the lore
of most of the prehistoric peoples who inhabited the raven's
circumpolar range in the Northern Hemisphere. Primitive art,
particularly that of the American Indians of the northwest
coast, shows a familiarity with raven behavior and anatomy that
has not been surpassed. I remember watching a Tlingit woman
in Juneau, Alaska, giving an evocative imitation of a raven walking and ruffling its feathers in a dance. At least one Indian tribe
professed to understand many of the raven's extremely varied,
often polysyllabic cries, so that a man might overhear raven con-
versations and thus learn what was afoot in the woods. (I can
well believe this. I've heard ravens calling back and forth as they
moved through heavy forest, and it reminded me of people carrying on a conversation from different rooms of a house. I also
noticed how raven "languages" changed, became more polysyllabic, as I traveled from California to southeast Alaska on a
hitchhiking trip, having nothing much to listen to except raven
talk as I stood beside the road for long hours.)

Modern science has produced raven statistics, which older
cultures did not have. We can go to a library and read that
ravens are the largest members of the order Passeriformes, the

perching birds, the bird group that includes three fifths of living species; that *Corvus corax,* the common raven, is 25 inches long and weighs 2 pounds; that ravens lay four to seven pale green, brown-spotted eggs in softly lined stick or bone (or even wire) nests in trees or on cliffs and abandoned buildings (including oil derricks and windmills in the desert). We can further learn that their American range includes western mountains south to El Salvador, most of Canada and Alaska, and wild parts of New England and Appalachia; that they live in some of the Northern Hemisphere's most hostile environments, including the Arctic coast and Himalayan peaks; that they are generally absent from some areas that seem more hospitable to us, such as farmland and temperate deciduous forest; and that they remain in the hostile environments they do favor virtually year-round, so that they are often the only birds—indeed the only life—to be found in certain wintry landscapes.

Our knowledge of ravens is systematic, then, but I doubt it's much deeper than our ancestors'. The only book I found under the subject heading Raven in the biology library of the University of California at Berkeley was a technical tome on certain aspects of raven muscalature. We know how many eggs the birds are likely to lay, but finding an actual raven's nest is another matter. The roost I've described has been known to exist since at least 1941, but ornithologists at a nearby bird observatory were unaware, as of 1979, of an authenticated raven nest site in the vicinity. We know that ravens prefer western mountains to eastern cornfields, but we don't know why. We know that ravens, as members of the Passeriformes, are among the most recently evolved of birds, the Passeriformes including the familiar songbirds as well as flycatchers, swallows, shrikes, and various exotic tropical families, but the implications of that knowledge are far from clear.

According to one faction of bird evolutionists, ravens, and members of the family Corvidae in general, are the most highly evolved of the passerines because of their considerable brain size. (Corvids have the largest cerebral hemispheres in relation to body size of all birds.) According to another faction, however, they are among the most primitive of the passerines because of their relatively unspecialized plumage. Each faction probably will enjoy its speculations undisturbed for some time because there's little evidence of how ravens, the Corvidae, or members of the order Passeriformes in general evolved. Archaeopteryx, the first known bird—the feathered, toothed creature that was fossilized so exquisitely in German Jurassic limestone—is the exception of bird fossils, not the rule. Feathers almost never fossilize, and hollow, delicate bird bones seldom do. Aquatic bird evolution is somewhat better known because ducks, grebes, herons, and other aquatic birds have relatively stout skeletons that tend to be entombed in the mud or sand of their waterside homes. But passerines are land birds, which usually die on land, where their skeletons are pulled apart by scavengers and nibbled away by rodents in search of calcium.

So we know little more of the specifics of how, when, and why ravens appeared on earth than did the Eskimos, who thought ravens swooped down from the heavens and created the earth. There are raven skeletons in the La Brea tar pits of southern California, where the birds died some 12,000 to 40,000 years ago along with saber-toothed cats, mastodons, ground sloths, and giant condors. Those fossil ravens are identical to the two species now inhabiting North America (the common *C. corax,* and the white-necked raven, *C. cyrptoleucus,* a smaller bird of the Southwest), and thus tell us nothing about raven origins or development.

We can always speculate, of course. The few fossils we have of passerines and corvids indicate that they had appeared by the Lower Tertiary Period, which ended about 20 million years ago. Subtropical forests and savannas covered today's temperate zone for most of that period, and raven ancestors may have inhabited those lush, warm regions. Ravens still have close relatives in Africa. As the global climate dried and cooled during subsequent epochs, those subtropical birds may have evolved the traits that suit ravens so well to today's mountains, deserts, and tundras—superb aerial skill for dealing with harsh and unpredictable winds, glossy black plumage for storing heat in frigid weather, highly developed communications skills for reporting scattered food sources, and quick wits and powerful beaks for exploiting those sources.

It is likely that the first small bands of humans who invaded the mountains, deserts, and tundra of the Northern Hemisphere found ravens in their present form, that invasion having taken place in the last brief second of evolutionary time. Those distant ancestors of ours would have been as impressed as we are by the raven's cleverness and aerial skills—probably more impressed, since they necessarily were more observant of such things. Their respect for ravens may have grown as they watched more majestic creatures pass away—saber-tooths, mastodons, giant condors—while ravens remained.

There are certain organisms that seem to have a stamp of permanence on them, that have evolved traits of a durability and economy that put them outside the usual timetable of extinction. Dinosaurs pass away, but the turtles that evolved with them remain; elephants dwindle, but opossums increase. The raven seems as likely a candidate for this stamp as any living bird. Ravens have been driven from parts of Eurasia and North America by modern civilization, but they seem to coexist with it quite comfortably in other parts (I've seen ravens in downtown San Francisco), and they are quick to reinhabit areas such as northern New England where the tide of civilization has receded somewhat. As long as deserts, mountains, and tundra produce rodents and insects, ravens will probably be around to eat them, and then to do contented somersaults in the chilly air.